362.83 Parker, Tony.
PAR

    In no man's land:
    some unmarried
    mothers

DATE			

79

In No Man's Land

Also by Tony Parker

The Twisting Lane—Some Sex Offenders
The Frying Pan—A Prison and Its Prisoners

Tony Parker

In No Man's Land
some unmarried mothers

DISCARD

Harper & Row, Publishers
NEW YORK, EVANSTON, SAN FRANCISCO, LONDON

FIRST U.S. EDITION

STANDARD BOOK NUMBER: 06-013276-0

LIBRARY OF CONGRESS CATALOG CARD NUMBER: 72-79684

For TOM
—who sees—
with love

Contents

I wonder if there are any links between unmarried mothers besides
the obvious ones? I do hope not.

(SALLY MORRISON)

CHAPTER ONE

FRANCESCA LAWTON

A lady is one who does what she ought, when she ought—and whether she wants to or not.

'The little one he sleeps now, Madame, so I go to my aunt tonight. The coffee-tray I leave on this table, yes?'

'Thank you, Lisette. Are you coming back?'

'Madame?'

'Tonight, I mean? Erm—revenez-vous ce soir?'

'Ah oui, Madame, certainement, je serai de revenir avant minuit.'

'Bien. Merci, bonsoir Lisette.'

Quietly the small plump au-pair girl slid the frosted-glass door of the sitting-room closed behind her. A few moments later the distant sound of the shutting of the flat door as she went out.

The tall young woman remained motionless, statuesque in the white linen caftan with its gold chain-link belt. Leaning with one shoulder against the wall at the end of the wide sweep of the fourth-floor balcony window, she looked out with delphinium-blue eyes at the pink and grey of the sunsetting sky, down at its reflection in the dulling water of the lake in the park below. Almond-shaped eyes in the smooth complexioned Botticellian face, the ash-blonde hair framing it falling loosely down on her shoulders. Occasionally, unhurriedly, she drew at the oval cigarette held lightly but firmly between the tips of long fingers.

Francesca Lawton always waited before she began to talk, always paused until the right moment; often for long, as though listening for some kind of signal inside her head to indicate that the correct time had come for unlocking words from their cage. She was twenty-two.

*

—The summer evenings after these long hot days are nice, aren't they? I like it from here when hardly anyone's left in the park. There's a, I think it's a mallard on the lake; she's got five or six chicks. Comes out when it's quiet, I've seen boys sometimes throwing stones. . . . A girl in jeans sitting on a bench under the willow over there reading a book. I wonder what it is . . . do you ever wonder what people are reading, if it's something you've read yourself? Gives you a guide as to what kind of person they are, they say. You were looking at those books weren't you, the other night, in my book-case. *The Sun King*, Nureyev's book, Durrell's *Alexandrian Quartet* . . . after you'd gone I thought what a misleading impression they could have given you. You didn't see the stacks of paper-backs, westerns and detective-stories, out of sight in the cupboard underneath. Then I thought no, not really misleading, I don't hide them deliberately; I prefer the hardcover books to be on the shelves, they look nicer. As long as you know the others are there. . . . I'm not what you might call an intellectual, more a person made up of bits and pieces, some of this and some of that. I suppose it's because I'm on the cusp. Astrology. But I don't believe in it, really. My birthdate makes me sometimes Sagittarian, sometimes a Capricornian; Sagittarians are supposed to be sociable, Capricornians are very shy—so that's true, contradictions, sometimes I'm one, sometimes the other. Coffee? White, two sugars, isn't it?

She moved slowly across the room, poured it out from the stainless-steel electric percolator, added cream from a small Georgian-design silver jug.

—I made a silly mistake last time, I can't think why. I told you we always stayed on holidays when I was little at a private hotel near St. David's Head owned by a Mrs. Patterson, didn't I? When I was talking to my mother on the 'phone last week I was telling her I'd been thinking about my early childhood and trying to remember the times we'd spent at Mrs. Patterson's, how we used to go scrambling over the rocks looking for sea-anemones in the little pools to tease with twigs. She said 'Fran, what *are* you talking about? We never stayed with Mrs. Patterson, she was just a woman we once met there. The woman who owned the hotel was called Mrs. Carlisle.'

But I haven't the faintest recollection of Mrs. Carlisle—who she was or what she looked like or anything, even though we must have stayed with her every year. Yet Mrs. Patterson, who she says we met just once, I'd recognise her immediately if I saw her now. Strange, isn't it? All this time I'd thought she was the woman who owned that hotel; it's not until we start prodding and poking about in my memory ... it's frightening a bit, I wonder how much else I've got wrong.

She said—my mother I mean—'Anyway, why are you wasting time on a long-distance 'phone-call gossiping about someone we've never seen before or since? Haven't you anything else to think about, I do hope you're going to start taking an interest in things outside again soon, weren't you going to join that amateur-dramatic society or something? You've got that girl to look after Simon now, surely you can begin going out a bit and doing something, can't you?'

Doing things is always the solution to problems as far as mother's concerned. Perhaps that's a bit unfair to her I suppose. It's just that we're ... values are different, aren't they, in different places to different people? Up north where she lives what matters is what you've got, and how much you've got of it. I suppose that's true here in the south too, if you really get down to it. It still clings to me, I suppose, surrounding myself with things. Those antique swords on the wall, that Persian shield, this big flat in a new block in one of the best residential areas; my car, my computerised washing-machine, the au pair, my clothes....

She stirred her coffee leisurely with a thin-stemmed gem-handled spoon, replaced it untasted on the table and lay back in the cushioned depths of the green velvet upholstered armchair. Sharply, suddenly, she shook her head.

—An effort to project myself from the present into the past. Where were we last time, where did we stop? Yes, that's right: when I was nine and went to boarding school. I'd say it was a very good school. The preparatory school before that, I told you that one was a nice school didn't I, well this was a good school. I suppose the difference is 'nice' means it's all right but they don't try to do much, and 'good' is when they pay more attention to your education.

It wasn't easy to get into—I don't mean academically because that didn't matter so much: what did matter was who you were, if your parents could afford the fees and who they knew. You had to be well-connected, as they say in the north—that meant monied-industrial, rather than aristocratic, though there were a few daughters of minor landed gentry in it too. If you got a daughter into Oakdale School, you really were somebody. Actually in fact I rather liked the idea of going because it had horses. That was the main attraction to me, I was very fond of horses; my father was a member of the local hunt, I often went riding. So to be going away to a school where they made a feature of the horses and the stables they had, at least according to the prospectus—well, that was something to be thrilled about; I never recollect any thoughts about not wanting to go away from home, no.

Somehow when I got there, the horses seem to disappear— in my memory, I mean. Perhaps they were important for a term or two, but I lost interest. 'Ruby', 'Musket', Sherbet' ... there must have been eight or nine, those are the only ones whose names I can remember though; old and barrel-shaped and dopey most of them, but thoroughly staid and reliable of course, and always beautifully kept. A phase most little girls go through, isn't it? It can't have lasted long in my case, I remember so little about them; I should think after the first year I hardly took any interest in the horses at all.

What was I interested in? Nothing much I suppose, would be the honest answer. What was I like? Oh, just ordinary. There were about sixty or seventy girls there, I was no different from any of the rest. Yes I suppose I must have been different, but I didn't feel it, I wasn't aware of it. There were three school 'Houses'—Markham, Dean and Grange. I was in Grange, that's the one that sticks in my mind for some reason. But then it might be like Mrs. Patterson, mightn't it? If I asked my mother she'd probably say 'Don't be ridiculous, Fran, you know perfectly well it was Markham.' She can remember more about me than I can, most parents are the same I should think. Anyway, three houses and I was in Grange, let's say; and it had ten or twelve dormitories, each quite small with only five or six girls in it. An old manor house, a country seat of some sort of lord or other, I've forgotten his name. It couldn't have been Lord Oakdale because the school wasn't named after a founder or anything like that. Its badge naturally was an acorn; one of the mistresses had composed the school song which was about mighty trees growing from tiny seeds, as you can imagine. It'd only been in existence I should think fifty years or less; but you got the feeling as soon as you went it'd been there for centuries. I don't remember much else about it, specially.

Oh yes, I know, the dormitories had got names like Howard, Norfolk, Maitland, Mowbray. And I was in ... gracious, which one was I in? Wait a minute, I remember now, yes of course: you didn't stay in one dormitory, you went into a different one each year, or every term possibly, though I can't think why. I know it was all systematic, perhaps it had something to do with what form you were in. No it wasn't, I think it had something to do with the family, the school family I mean. Yes, that was it. They had a big thing about it not being just a school, it was a family; everybody belonged to the family, we ate together and did everything together, you were moved round from one dormitory to another so that none was ever 'your' dormitory, everything was 'ours'. Yes, that's right, that's what it was.

I don't remember much else about it ... it was in the heart of some beautiful countryside. The nearest town was an hour's 'bus-ride away, you could only go there on a Saturday afternoon, there always had to be at least four of you together, and you had to wear school uniform if you went. The food was all right; I suppose I'd remember if it'd been particularly good or particularly bad. The lessons were the usual, I wasn't top of the form or bottom, I didn't excel at anything and I wasn't dreadful at anything ... you had to write a letter home once a week. One of the mistresses was called Miss Barnstaple, or was it Miss Taunton ... no, it must have been Barnstaple. There was a bit of emphasis on religion but not much, Sundays you had to be quiet and well-behaved, there was a school service in the evening. A clock on the tower in the courtyard, it never said anything but ten-past-two; when you first looked you thought it'd only got one hand, actually there were two only they were caught together and nobody'd ever done anything about it. There was a small lake in the grounds, you weren't supposed to swim in it but of course we did, the water was filthy dirty, I couldn't do it now.... A cat, a ginger cat that was always around the place ... we went for walks in the country sometimes....

What else now, let me think ... if you missed the two o'clock 'bus on Saturday there wasn't another till four; you had to be back in school by five o'clock anyway so there was no point in catching it, because all it did when it got to the town was turn round and come back.

Lots of games, rounders, hockey, netball ... cocoa before you went to bed, you changed into your night things and then had your cocoa.... Somebody died, one of the mistresses, but it was in the holidays conveniently. Sunlight in the summer, snow sometimes in the winter, the lake froze once I remember.... That's it, that's about all: nothing exceptional. It's not very inspiring; I told you I've an absolutely dreadful memory. Then after that school, I——

Happy? Yes of course, I expect so. Happy, unhappy, I don't really remember. I would've done if I'd been particularly one or the other I suppose. I remember games were what I liked best, those were my happiest memories. I was very good at them, particularly rounders and netball and hockey—in fact I was captain of our house-team in all three of them. I suppose I could say I had a natural ability for games, but not for anything much else, at least not for the first few years I was there. It was only when I got up into the higher forms round about when I was fifteen and sixteen that I started enjoying taking much interest in actual school work. But that wasn't the main purpose of the school anyway, you weren't sent there to be turned into a brilliant scholar and go to a university. You were sent because it was a good school where you would learn how to grow up into a lady.

Oh yes, that's one thing I do remember very clearly; we were told at least once a week at morning assembly, and on any and every suitable occasion in between. Yes, it was most clearly described and explained, and always in exactly the same words. My memory might be vague about everything else, but that much at least is still perfectly clear.

Silence; the room greying with shadow as the evening slowly collapsed. Comfortably she had sunk further and further down almost horizontal in the armchair; with her legs crossed at the knee she lifted one foot to the level of her eyes and stared expressionlessly at it, watching her blue velvet slipper expand and contract with the curling and uncurling of her toes. Sinuously she had raised one arm upwards as she stretched,

the wide sleeve of her caftan fallen down from it to her
shoulder; and while she talked at the hinge of her wrist her
hand slowly rose and fell, and fell and rose, and rose and
fell.

—I can see Miss Robinson our Headmistress standing there
saying it now. It was a simple but very exact definition, I've
always thought. 'A lady is one who does what she ought, when
she ought—and whether she wants to or not.'

*

A long drive home, late at night, and dark. No, she had said,
she wasn't a great reader of poetry. She had read some at
school, the established poets of course, the well-known ones;
but not now, no, she hardly ever read any poetry at all. The
moderns? No, she didn't really know any of them. Stevie
Smith, vaguely she'd heard of him, she thought, if it was a
him, or was it a her? Why, particularly, was there some special
reason for my asking? Oh no, no; no. A long drive home, late
at night, and dark.

> '... I was much further out than you thought
> And not waving but drowning ...
> Oh, no, no, no, it was too cold always ...
> I was much too far out all my life
> And not waving but drowning.'

*

The flat had cost £20,000. Her net weekly income from
privately inherited personal trust funds and their investments
after deduction of tax, was almost £50. Her car was a white
Triumph Vitesse, her perfume was Balenciaga's 'Quadrille',
her cigarettes a Turkish brand which few tobacconists stocked
and most had never heard of. Holidays, well she said, they
varied: cruises, North Africa, Venice, the Adriatic. Clothes?
A fairly good selection, yes, she wasn't by any means clothes-
mad but if she saw something she particularly liked she went
in and tried it on, and if it suited her she bought it. She supposed it would be true to say, yes, that she could have anything, more or less, if she wanted it.

—Which is one of the things, really you see, isn't it? Well it can make life a bit difficult as far as your relationships with others are concerned. Yes, by others I do mean particularly men; having money is very much an additional complication. Well, additional to my looks. I wouldn't call myself a raving beauty; but men do look at me, it'd be silly to pretend they didn't and that I wasn't aware of it. You know after you've passed him that somebody's turned his head, even though you can't see him doing it; I can't explain how but a woman just does. Somewhere like Italy they don't even make any pretence, though I know they do it all the time with women there of course. Madame ... what was it, 'Madonna bella, che belleza!' —that was in a restaurant, a complete stranger. But then all Italians are supposed to be like that aren't they?

There are a lot of complications, really, all round, that I have to try and think about, one way and another. It's Lisette's day off today; I've brought the percolator in here, I'll just switch it on, it shouldn't take long.

Last time it was the boarding school wasn't it, from nine to sixteen, and I told you all there was about that, at least as much as I remember. There was something else I thought of after you'd gone, but I've forgotten it again so I suppose it can't have been all that important. And before that we fairly well covered up to the age of nine, anything about it I could think of. But what I did remember about that, about the family holidays for instance, I got wrong, didn't I; all that business about Mrs. Patterson and who really owned the private hotel at St. David's Head. You must get tired of me saying 'I can't remember, I don't remember.' I do try to think, but I don't seem able to do it, I can't keep things in my head—like that idea I had after you'd gone last time, and now it's completely gone again.

I think it was something to do with ... it was because of something you asked me when you were going, I was thinking about it afterwards and it reminded me of something else: I thought yes, I must try and remember to tell you about it, about the boarding school I think it was. Well anyway it's gone, it doesn't matter.

So I left Oakdale at seventeen, and ... poetry—that's right, you did, you asked about poetry, of course that's it. I wasn't a great reader of it I said, except for what we'd had to do for school work. That was it, that was what I'd been thinking of, it reminded me, yes of course. The point was, poetry isn't something I read now or ever have done, much; but what I did read, I mean at school, when I come to start thinking about it I realise it had a profound effect on me at the time; in fact it must have been in a sense quite a sort of formative thing, at least as far as religion is concerned.

I'm not putting it very clearly, but there was a definite change in me then, about the one definite change I suppose I've ever had, and it was all due to poetry. Up till the time we're talking about, in my mid-teens in school, for some reason I've not been able to fathom I'd never given a thought to the subject of God or religion or belief of any kind at all. I didn't have any religious ideas whatsoever, I think I must have been born a natural heathen. My parents weren't particularly church-going, and all that business at school I was telling you about, Sunday evening services and prayers, made no impression on me at all. I hadn't thought out an atheist position, nothing like that: it's just there was a total blank, a nothing, a kind of assumption it'd all got nothing to do with me.

When we did have to start reading English lit. for exams in the fifth and sixth form, it was funny but some kind of religious thinking began to start up inside me. Certain things, certain poems particularly, weren't just pieces to be studied: they had a terrific effect on me personally. Well particularly Thomas Hardy's 'The Darkling Thrush', I don't know if you know it. It's about how he hears this bird on a gate, singing on a cold dreary winter's evening; and there's absolutely nothing as far as he can see, in the landscape or on earth anywhere, for it to sing about. I can't recall the exact words, but Hardy said something to the effect that it started him thinking there must be something, or somebody, I think he called it a 'blessed hope', somehow and somewhere in the world that he himself was unaware of.

That was exactly my position, it struck a key, I can remember thinking 'Good gracious, it's almost what I might have written if I could ever have found the words.' Then I went on from there to Wordsworth; I don't mean discovered him for myself, his poems were another one of the set books we had to do. In 'The Excursion', he describes the universe as being like a sort of sea-shell held up to the ear of Faith. In other words if you listen you hear—that all nature's part of one whole, there's a kind of unity and totalness in everything. Human beings, nature, eternity, God, whatever—they're all one. I don't know if I've explained it very well, but it made me convinced there must be a God.

I suppose that makes me some kind of Christian, though I don't know exactly what. But I do have the belief still, and it's an important part of me. Not as a hope or a consolation, a better life in the hereafter or anything like that; just a believer in God. But not to any purpose, if that doesn't sound ridiculous. I never think God will get me out of anything, or make things any better, or there's much point in prayer or going to church. But I do think there is a God. In fact I know there is.

I suppose I ought to go on and think it out more, consider the implications and so on. Perhaps I will one day. But I'm not very good at that, and anyway I'm not conscious of being stuck or frustrated because I haven't got any further. All I did want to say was it was there, that belief, and still is. Nothing that's happened since has given me any cause to change it.

I mean, out there—you know I often just stand at the window and look out at the lake—whatever I see, whether it's the ducks, or school-boys sitting on the bank fishing or throwing stones, or an old couple side by side on one of the benches by the path, or the trees, the elders and the limes and the beeches, or the clouds in the sky, the buildings of the town in the distance ... they're all part of one thing, all part of God if you know what I mean. I should think that coffee's perked enough now, wouldn't you, how strong do you like it?

Well at Oakdale eventually I took six—was it six or five, no it was six—'O' levels in English Literature, English Language, French, German, History and Geography; and then I went on and did 'A' level French and German. What did I want to do after? To be perfectly honest, I hadn't a clue—or at least for a long time I hadn't. I knew I wasn't going to university, I never had any thought of doing it, or more correctly my parents had got no ideas of that kind. They weren't ambitious for me academically and they hadn't encouraged me to be either, because my future was already mapped out for me anyway.

It was very straightforward; as I told you, I was going to be a lady. That meant being at Oakdale to learn how, then going

on to a finishing-school on the Continent for a year or so.
Then I suppose I would have travelled for a while to see a few
different places in the world; and then I'd be 21. At that point I
would come into the inheritance: this was family money tied
up in trusts and things, that had all been arranged ages ago by
my father and grandfather. As I was the only child surviving
at the end of the family line, all of it would come to me.

So there presumably I would be at twenty-one; well brought
up, expensively educated, travelled and comfortably off. I
presume I was going to make a good marriage if someone
suitable could be found, which would be somebody who wasn't
a fortune hunter, perhaps the son of one of my father's
connections. I remember during holidays towards the end of
my time at school how pleased my father was with me. He
used to show off to his friends, what a nicely brought up
daughter he had. He was very proud: he'd been a hard-
working business man all his life, built up the family engineering firm to the point where when he retired it was going to be
sold for a good price to one of the big Northern business
consortiums. Now his daughter was blossoming into an eligible
marrying proposition. If I'd been a boy I suppose I'd have
followed him into the firm. But he hadn't got a son, he'd only
got me; so he was making the best of that.

It wasn't his fault it didn't work out. There was nothing
more he could have done, nothing he ought to have done that
he hadn't. The future should have been just as he planned. I
suppose it would have been too, if I hadn't got this idea in my
head, suddenly and quite unremovably, during my last year at
school ... gracious, I've been rambling on, I hadn't noticed
how dark it was getting. I must turn the lights on. Excuse
me.

Talking, she got up from her chair and moved idly across
the room; touching the wall with her hand she felt vaguely
backwards behind her, fumbling for the edge of the framework
round the frosted glass sliding door.

—Heaven knows where the idea had come from, because I
don't know; out of nowhere. But it suddenly descended on me
with absolute conviction and certainty, just like that.

Her hand found the switch and pressed it. From the two
glittering multi-bulbed chandeliers which hung from the ceil-

ing, from the eight wall lamps round the room with their white
conical shades, from the concealed fluorescent strip lighting
beneath the pelmet fitted round the curve of the bay window
from one end to the other above the tangerine velvet curtains.
Light.

—I wanted to go on the stage. A shy person like me. I mean
really, can you imagine it? Oh, honestly, please don't worry
about it, Simon's always knocking cups over on the floor,
that's why I've got this chocolate-brown carpet, spilled coffee
won't show up on it at all, really it won't.

*

Last time I was telling you about the upset I caused, wasn't
I, that fantastic notion about going on the stage, which
changed the plans for my life which my parents had taken for
granted, and worked at so hard. I said it'd come out of the
blue, but I suppose that's not quite true, because we had put
on a few plays at school and I'd done a bit of verse-speaking in
House Drama Festivals, and once or twice in outside competitions too. I was quite good, particularly at elocution, I won
one or two prizes and awards at local competitions, so I
suppose that's what gave me the idea.

When I said after Oakdale I wanted to go to London to
drama school and learn how to become an actress, I don't
think my parents quite knew what to do. My father was
always one for avoiding direct confrontations: he preferred to
sit quiet until things turned out the way he intended, which
they usually did. So he was very sensible and didn't try to
make an issue out of it. Knowing the kind of man he is,
businesslike and shrewd, now I come to think of it he must
have made a few enquiries himself and known what the outcome would be when I applied to the drama school I had in
mind. They said I wasn't old enough to go; I couldn't start till
I was eighteen. By that time it would be after the first year of
their course had started, so I'd have to wait until the following
year.

I'm sure my father must have found that out before I did. So
far as he was concerned plans for my finishing school education on the Continent would go ahead. I expect he thought that
by the time that was complete, my enthusiasm for a stage

career would have died a natural death. He knew I wasn't a particularly determined character who laid long-term plans and carried them through, any more than I am now.

So I went to Germany instead, to what's called a *tochter-heim* near Bonn. Why particularly a German finishing-school I don't know; I presume it would be something to do with my father's European business connections. It was small, expensive and select. There were only twenty girls there, so the fees must have been fairly substantial to make it pay.

About half of them were German and the other half foreign —two from America, one from France, another English girl whose parents were something to do with the Malaysian Government, a South African, an Australian, I think two South American girls and a Danish girl ... was she Danish or Swedish, Inge was her name, no I'm fairly certain she was Danish.

It was really a rather horrid place, I didn't care for it at all. I didn't like any of the other girls there, nor did they like me. I presume they thought me stand-offish: I don't think I was really, it was just that I was shy. And I was beginning to change my character, changing inside myself somehow, though probably only subconsciously. From what to what though, that's something I don't know. From a well brought up, nicely mannered young English lady into a, well I was going to say rebel but that's too strong a word. I wasn't a revolutionary or a non-conformer, and I certainly didn't go wild and kick over the traces or anything. It was just that all the things that I'd been sent to finishing-school to learn seemed utterly boring and pointless. I can't say I like Germans much anyway, they're so meaninglessly formal. Even to such a conventional English young lady as I was, all that bowing and decorous introductions, handshakes with the men standing to attention.... Heavens, even the 'bus conductors in Germany are like soldiers; more like soldiers even than actual British soldiers are.

What did we do all the time, oh everything we did was quite pointless and stupid. There was a three-week rota, one week you did needlework, one week you did cookery, and one week you did housecraft and deportment. Then you started back at Week One again, and it went on and on like that, that's all.

Needlework included sewing, dressmaking, mending and

embroidery. Cookery was supposed to be dishes and how to prepare them, German recipes of course, but those like me whose German wasn't very good and couldn't follow the instructions inevitably got jobs like peeling potatoes, cutting up vegetables and doing the washing-up. Housecraft included laying tables, setting cutlery in the correct order, which wine you served with what dish, exactly what shape of wine glasses you put different wines in, and what temperature they had to be at; how to make serviettes into roses, who went in and in what order of preference to the dining-room, and where they sat at the table in relation to the hostess. And on top of that was deportment, which was how to conduct yourself when you went out, depending on where you were, who you were with, and what the situation was.

Of course these were German ideas that were taught, German society standards; as I say it was all ghastly and boring. Every evening there was dinner; you had to dress for it as though it was a formal occasion. If your dress wasn't right or your accessories were wrong, you got black looks and corrections pointed out to you in front of everybody else at table. The evening meals used to cause more bad feeling than any other single thing in the curriculum. That's another reason why I said I don't care for Germans much. All the standards were German, and I suppose it's a matter of fundamental difference of approach. For formal dinners German women tend to dress 'up', while in most other European countries, unless it's a charity ball or something, I think women on the whole prefer to dress 'down'. I don't mean they don't make themselves look smart, because they do, and put a lot of effort into it. But as far as the old Frau in charge of the *tochterheim* was concerned, being smart meant plastering yourself with everything you'd got, decking yourself out to look like a Christmas tree. Simplicity was a word she'd never heard of, nor the French expression 'chic'. The idea of a woman appearing in a simple black dress with a single pearl pendant from a chain at the front, and to my mind looking extremely elegant and smart, was simply not her way of looking at things at all.

We—all the foreigners that is—were always getting into trouble for not making any effort, according to her opinion. The French girl there really did look like an illustration from a fashion magazine sometimes. I remember one week in dressmaking she made herself a beautiful lime green dress with a high square neckline and three-quarter length sleeves, and spent hours pinning it, putting little darts in so that the bustline was perfect, the waistline, the hemline, everything: a beautiful kind of shot silk with a kind of changing-colour effect. She wore it dead plain, her black hair scraped back and fastened in a pony tail with a matching band of tiny beryls, but not a scrap of make-up or lipstick or anything. She looked marvellous, she was only a tiny little thing about so high. And for that, all she got was angry words about having no idea of taste, from this mountain of pink flesh Frau in black lace with diamanté clips and bracelets at the top of the table.

Gracious, they were terrible, those evening meals. And after them we then had to 'socialise' for two hours. That meant sitting drinking coffee, not forgetting to hold the cups correctly, smoking two cigarettes and no more, and making polite conversation with each other in German. If any of us tried to talk about something between ourselves, in English or French, we were pulled up and told to speak German. I loathed it all....

No, to be honest there was just one thing during that period I enjoyed, which was when we went on trips up into the mountains sometimes for a week's ski-ing. That really was fabulous: the scenery, the forests, the snow. We had a lot of fun. And of course as you got better at it, you enjoyed it even more and more.

It gave us the rare opportunity to meet a few men too, either boys who were on the slopes ski-ing themselves, or the instructors. But I don't know what it is about ski-ing instructors, they all seem to regard themselves as God's gift to women. At the après-ski parties we were allowed to go to occasionally, they were simply awful; they took it for granted you wanted nothing so much as an opportunity to go to bed with them: that was all you had come for, why else should you be up there in the mountains?

Like all assumptions I suppose it was based on something, it must have been true with a certain type of woman. What annoyed me was they thought it applied to everyone, all women of every age. That was the only thing that ever caused any trouble between that Danish girl Inge and me. She was my friend there, we shared a room all the time I was at the *tochterheim.* Her outlook on sex was I suppose typically Scandinavian: if she liked a man, she went to bed with him. Accompanied by a very carefully vetted German boy, once a month we were allowed to go to a small dancing club. You could hardly call it a night-club, but at least there were members of the opposite sex there, and so long as Frau had given her permission you could stay out until about quarter past ten.

What had I started saying ... oh yes, about Inge. Well there were times when she and I were allowed out together with two boys chosen from the local military academy. More than once, I never saw her again for the whole of the rest of the evening; then she'd arrive back at the dancing club just before the time when we had to return to the school. She was absolutely blatant about it, what she'd been doing and how much she'd enjoyed it, how much better or worse this one had been as a lover than the previous one, chattering away as though she'd been for a swim or something. I used to get furious, I was really disgusted at her being so promiscuous.

She must have done it at least three times in the year I was there, if not four. Yes I do think that's promiscuous, most certainly. I was eighteen at that time, eighteen and a half perhaps; I'd only ever even been kissed twice, and one of those times had been by a ski-ing instructor who like all the others made a grab at anyone that happened to be within range.

I quite definitely had the idea in my mind, coming as I did from my background and upbringing and schooling, that virginity was something precious to be protected at all costs until I was married. Though I must say I never had the slightest difficulty, or felt I was in danger of losing it: no emotion which might have led in that direction had ever affected me....

—Oh, Simon, she said, as the frosted glass door slid open with a bump and a fair curly-haired boy, 18 months old in a buttoned-up pyjama suit, tottered smiling sleepily into the room. Now whatever are you doing out of bed at this time of night, eh? Did something wake you up? It's long past time you were fast asleep, whatever would Lisette say if she saw you? Come on, back to bed now, say 'Good night', that's it and kiss Mummy good night, Mummy'll put you back with Baa-lamb and Elephant and then you can snuggle down again and go to sleep and in the morning we'll ...

*

She had a table-model cigarette lighter of plain white porcelain, shaped like an egg, that pulled apart in the middle. Often after using it she closed it and held it between her fingers and stroked it, or sometimes cupped it gently in the palm of her hand.

—It's very beautiful, very satisfying I think. I've always loved beautiful things, I don't like anything that's ugly or ill-proportioned. I can't stand any kind of physical deformity or defect in people either, I have to turn my head away, I can't look at them. It's an egg obviously, but it also reminds me of snow: it's shaped like a curve blown in the snow by the wind, isn't it? It's symmetrical like nature: natural shapes made by the elements are always perfect in design, have you noticed? It's cool like snow too, sometimes I like to hold it against my cheek.

When I came back from Germany I never wanted to go abroad again. My father was surprised, at least he said rather mildly he was surprised. I should think in actual fact he was flabbergasted that I hadn't given up my idea of being on the stage and was still going to pursue it. Not having raised any objections the previous year when I wrote to the drama school in London, there was nothing much he could do when I applied again, nor when they accepted me. All he kept saying, all through the summer before I went, was 'Fran, are you *sure* that's what you want to do?'

It was: so arrangements were made for me to live in a hostel for girls. I should think it was most carefully vetted by my parents before I was allowed to set foot in it, but eventually off I went.

It wasn't a very good drama school, nothing like RADA, not in that kind of class. It was small and exclusive and with high fees naturally: nearly all the staff I suppose were failed actors and actresses who'd settled for a quiet life and an undemanding job and none of them were well known. My parents paid me an allowance. Again I went through an uneventful period there, in which nothing memorable of any kind happened, with one exception. Quite by chance one day I was in one of the big London post offices, buying a letter-card to write home, and standing right next to me in the queue was a girl whose face looked vaguely familiar. Then it suddenly struck me. 'Good heavens,' I said, 'Aren't you Elizabeth Manning who used to be at Oakdale?' 'That's right,' she said, 'I am. And you're—gracious, you're Francesca Lawton!'

We went off and had a cup of coffee, and it was really most odd. We hadn't been particularly close friends at school, but obviously we'd both changed a lot and we found we got on terrifically well. I asked what she was doing in London, she had some kind of job as a translator of textbooks, I think. She was doing quite well, but that particular day she was very worried because she'd been sharing a flat with another girl who'd just got a job abroad and was going to leave. Elizabeth didn't know how she was going to find another person to share the flat, she said, because she didn't know many people and she didn't want just anybody. 'I don't suppose you're looking for somewhere to live, are you?' she said.

I wasn't, and I'd never given any thought to trying to find somewhere of my own, because I'd taken it for granted my parents wouldn't agree, and I was financially dependent on them. But sharing a flat with a girl from Oakdale would be a different matter. So I used the letter-card that I'd just bought to write and ask them could I go in with Elizabeth and would they increase my allowance so I could afford it?

Naturally my father and mother came down to London to have a look at the flat, and I presume to have a look at Elizabeth too. But as well as being an Oakdale girl she was the daughter of one of my father's acquaintances so that was all right, and a couple of weeks later I moved in with her. It was a nice flat, quite big, we had a room each and a sitting-room and a dining-room and so on.

Then it came to Easter, or was it Whitsun ... no, that's right, I think it was Easter. I went home for the holidays, and I'd said if we were going away I still didn't want to go abroad again; so knowing how much I'd enjoyed the ski-ing in Germany my parents had arranged for us to spend two weeks at a hotel in the Grampians up near Glenshee. That was where I met Philip.

He was a ski-ing instructor, and exactly like all the others I'd come across in Germany. He was terrifically handsome and good-looking, blond curly hair, sun-tanned, physically perfect. Philip ... gracious, I can't remember his other name now, what was it, Philip Martin, Philip Marshall—yes, that's it, Marshall. By the way, I suppose I'd better make it clear at this point that he is or rather that he was eventually the father of Simon.

I liked him during the holiday, he was good company, but as I say, I'd had experience of other ski-ing instructors and he was certainly no different; any girl or all girls, whoever happened to be handy. I didn't encourage him in any way, and nothing whatsoever happened between us, and I wasn't heartbroken when the holiday was over, nothing like that. As far as I was concerned there were no thoughts of keeping in touch with him afterwards, let alone ever meeting him again.

I came back to London at the end of the holidays and went on at the drama school. I was beginning to find it rather a bore, and it had certainly disillusioned me as far as wanting a stage career was concerned, which I think was probably what my father knew would happen. April, May, June ... then one night there was a ring at the flat door-bell. Elizabeth was out, I went and opened it, and there was Philip. How on earth he'd found out where I lived I haven't the remotest idea.

I asked him in, I think perhaps I was a bit flattered that out of all the girls that had passed through his hands, literally, he should have remembered me and come to see me. He was up in London for a few days he said, because he was starting in business with a friend, they were going to run an indoor ski-ing school with some kind of selling sporting goods equipment as a sideline as well.

When he started after ten minutes to kiss me and try to make love to me, I was really taken aback. I wasn't excited, but in a strange kind of way I was curious, as though this was something happening to somebody else and I was interested to see how it went. It didn't, as a matter of fact, because Elizabeth came back before long.

He came round the next night, and the next night, and the night after that. He had a flat himself, which he was sharing with two or three other boys, and he was always inviting me to go round there one evening, and eventually I went. He wouldn't give up trying to get me into bed with him then, he was very persistent, very determined. And I think I'd more or less made up my mind that if he kept on I'd let him, because of this curiosity to see what it was like. And that was how it took place. He used to get me on his bed; sometimes on the table by the side of it there were hairpins, and when I saw them I'd wonder detachedly who it had been the night before.

I think it was a total of three times altogether that we had sexual intercourse. It did nothing at all to me, just a disillusioning experience as far as I was concerned. I'd read about it in books, it's supposed to be wonderful isn't it, chimes of bells ringing, avalanches; but it was nothing like that at all. Pure curiosity: and I'd found out it was nothing, and that was all there was to it.

I went home for the summer vacation; that year we went on a Mediterranean cruise, I think, yes that's right we did. Then one day during it I thought it was funny, I was sure I should have had a period, it must have been weeks since the previous one. So it dawned on me I must be pregnant. I wasn't alarmed or worried, I didn't think much about it, it seemed quite meaningless. I put it out of my mind again until the end of the holiday and then I went back to London.

When I told Philip he just shrugged. He said 'Well, it's not the first time it's happened.' I think at the time I took it he meant to other girls in general; but now I suppose he must have meant it more specifically, in the sense that it wasn't the first time it had happened with him. There was an immediate noticeable cooling-off on his part, then a really rapid loss of interest in me.

I didn't know what I should do, and didn't know anybody I could talk to whose advice I could ask. Certainly not my parents; that was unthinkable. But eventually I told Elizabeth, and she was really very good; she made enquiries to see if there was any way I could get rid of it, and after a time found a woman doctor who said she'd examine me. Oh, meanwhile I'd left the drama school. I gave my parents the excuse I didn't want to go on the stage any more, so continuing there would be a waste of their money and my effort. I thought I'd perhaps try to get myself a job, though doing what I hadn't any idea.

This all took time, weeks were going by; when I got round to the woman doctor at last, she told me I was too far on for abortion. She put me in touch with the Moral Welfare people, I think they call themselves 'Wel-Care' now. Their social worker was splendid, not a bit preachery or attitudinising, just quietly practical when it came to arranging a hospital bed for me, getting me to go to the ante-natal clinic and that sort of thing.

She said she thought I ought to tell my parents, and I went home at Christmas fully intending to if the opportunity arose. But it didn't. I've never had much contact with my parents somehow. There were a lot of friends and relatives in the house as usual over Christmas and New Year, and I never got a chance, or when I did the moment didn't seem quite right. I was very small, I must have been carrying the baby right back inside me; apart from an odd remark when I arrived, my mother saying how well I was looking and she was glad I was putting on a bit of weight at last, no one noticed anything.

So I came back to London without having said anything. It was only about eight or nine weeks later that Simon was born. Odd, isn't it? Up till then I'd thought after he was born I'd have him adopted; but after actually having him, and looking after him in hospital, there was no question of it. If anyone had asked me before, or I'd ever thought about it, I'd have said without hesitation I was going to give him for adoption.

That was another way the Wel-Care social worker was so good. She never tried to influence me, simply told me what alternatives there were and left it to me to make up my own mind. When I decided afterwards I would try and get a job, and did in fact get a small temporary one more or less to keep myself occupied, she helped me find a foster-mother I could leave Simon with, and then another one again when that didn't work out. She was really marvellous.

I had rather a difficult time for a few months: Elizabeth had had to give up the flat because she got a new job in the Midlands. I couldn't afford to keep it on by myself, let alone with Simon. I still wasn't quite twenty-one by a few months, so I'd no money to play about with, which meant there'd have to be a few gap-bridging arrangements.

There seemed no sense in going on not telling my parents, particularly as they were beginning to mention our next sum-

mer holidays in their letters, asking me where I'd like to go. So
I plucked up courage and went home for the week-end. I
didn't take Simon with me; as soon as I got them alone after
the friends who'd been there had departed, I told them quite
straightly and simply. They were surprised, and I think a bit
hurt that I hadn't told them that I was pregnant at Christmas.
But it was a *fait accompli*, there was nothing much they could
say. They kept the news absolutely to themselves, presuming I
was going to have it adopted when I went back to London I
suppose. They didn't ask me questions at all; who the father
was, or anything. I came back to London for a few more
weeks, then I rang them up and said I was coming home for
another week-end. That time I took Simon with me; I told
them I'd made up my mind to keep him, if I could find somewhere decent in London to live, and work out a way of
financing myself.

My father said very little, but only made a practical suggestion: that he'd make me a loan which would carry me
through in reasonably comfortable furnished accommodation
until my next birthday which would be the one when I came
into the money from the trusts. Which in fact is what he did,
and when the time came I got the money and bought this
place, and here I am. Which brings us up to the present day,
doesn't it?

Tired, she sat upright in the arm-chair, her back straight, her
face expressionless, her voice as always softly modulated and
her words low and clear. She opened the egg-shaped lighter, lit
another cigarette with it, and then put it quietly down on the
table, spinning it round gently with one finger.

—A rather factual narrative I'm afraid, not a lot to be made
of it. Perhaps you'd care for some more coffee, would you?

*

Many times when Francesca talked in the summer's fading
evenings in the lessening light her eyes' deep blueness hardened
into opacity; sometimes she would sit on the big settee in the
curve of the balcony window and often be silent there for a

long time, cupping her chin in her hand as she looked at the sky with her feet curled up underneath her and the thinly-spiralling cigarette smoke wreathing slowly above her head.

Outside, once, an incessant cascade of bitter rain made a mockery of what had started high with promise of another long lingering end to a sunlit day.

A black tailored trouser-suit, with the gold-buttoned jacket flared at the waist; by her on one of the thick cushions of the settee a large maroon leather photograph album, the cover gilt-embossed. She turned back through the leaves inside it, page after black page of snapshots, each neatly annotated in white ink underneath. 'Q.E. II leaving Southampton, view from stern.' 'Casablanca, street market.' 'Venice, fountain in monastery courtyard.' 'Thalsang, near Bonn, ski-lift.' On earlier pages, 'Front of our house.' 'Orchard and part of the garden.' 'Me at St. David's; aged 7.'

—My childhood, all my life as it was, as it is and goes on. Still a lot of pages to fill. I wonder what they'll have on them eventually. Or do I wonder ... no I don't suppose I do, not really very much. I don't often think about tomorrow, hardly ever in fact. I suppose that's my trouble. But then I don't really think about today either ... no, nor yesterday. I told you I've a bad memory, I don't recollect things easily. Not that there's much to remember: no more than there is to think about if I start trying to wonder about tomorrow.

Yes, there are a few places where photographs have been taken out; blank spaces, a person I don't care to remind myself exists, or have to explain about him to other people. I suppose one day when Simon gets older he'll start looking at the album, won't he ... I wonder what I shall say to him. About photographs it's easy enough, 'Oh it was just a friend, she wanted it so I gave it back to her.' I wonder what I shall say to him when he starts to ask the other things though: I haven't given it a thought yet. I won't either, I don't suppose, until I have to. He's what, eighteen months now, nearly two; he's bound to begin asking questions one day. What should I do, make up a tale, tell him a lie? Say his father's dead, which he is to all practical intents and purposes. ... I suppose one day I shall have to think what I ought to say, and when I ought to. On the whole I usually tend to say the first thing which comes into my head.

She fingered the thick gold band she wore on her wedding-ring finger, held her hand out in front of her, turning it slowly from one side to the other.

—Well, I wear this ring naturally, because of where I live, here in this area I mean. It says 'Mrs. Lawton' on the name-plate by the bell downstairs at the entrance to the block, you'll have noticed. To the au pair, my husband is abroad on business for the company he works for; that's where he'll stay until it begins to be embarrassing, then it's very simple, I get another au pair. Also I wear it as a measure of protection; yes, against men, particularly the type who if they found out I was an unmarried mother would regard it as some kind of public announcement, more or less an open invitation to start making advances.

No, I'll never get married, no. Almost certainly I'd say quite definitely not. No, I wouldn't marry Philip even if he did re-appear and ask me to. That's hardly likely anyway: the last time I heard of him, which must be two years ago now nearly, he'd gone to Canada. Presumably opportunities for running ski-ing schools and sports goods businesses are better there. I've never seen him since the time I was pregnant; and I've no wish to. It doesn't worry me, now I sometimes have difficulty even in remembering his name.

I've had no other boy-friend since that time. No one, noth-ing of any kind. I've neither been to bed nor had intercourse with any other man, either before or since, nor any wish to. The odd man I've met who even so much as hinted interest in that sort of thing just by his tone of voice perhaps, or a slight look in his eyes, I've always made it perfectly clear immedi-ately that he'd better turn his attention elsewhere.

I'm always suspicious of what a man wants. I don't meet many of course under the circumstances, but those around my own age haven't got anything like the same amount of money, for a start. So I can never be sure what it is they're after—is it me, or is it my money? As for those in what you might call the same social bracket, well I've gone right against the accepted code as far as they're concerned. They can get a much nicer girl, one with no strings attached. Who isn't in my position.

Who hasn't done what I've done, or at least if she has, has been much cleverer at doing something about it. One who hasn't, well, you know; in perfectly straight terms, one who hasn't got herself an illegitimate baby.

If I did marry, what sort of a man do I imagine he would be? The simple answer is I don't: I don't imagine, I mean. I don't think about it, I don't think about the future or the present or the past as I said before. In fact I don't think, full stop.

I suppose because as far as marriage is concerned, presumably that must have something to do with love, or being in love or words to that effect. Quite honestly I haven't the remotest idea what the word means. I've never experienced it. It's true I love Simon; and I must love my parents I suppose; and I presume they love me. But not in that way; that sort of love, the other sort, I know nothing about it.

If a man did say he loved me ... I must think, or try to. I'm never very good at thinking, I never seem able to put my feelings into thoughts. I beg your pardon? I said I'm never very good at putting my feelings into words. ...

I suppose I would look him in the eye and say 'What do you mean by love? In fact you don't mean love, you mean lust; lust for my body, physical carnal desire, that's what you mean by love. You don't want me, you want my body, and you think that the way to get it is to tell me you love me.' Or words to that effect. Though I'm sure I wouldn't be able to be quite so eloquent about it.

But my reaction would be that one, yes, it would be that immediately and emphatically, quite instinctively. I think all men really do just lust after women's bodies, that's what they want and nothing else; and of course with me there's the money thing as well, which makes me still more suspicious. Give a man a chance then, to prove otherwise? No, I wouldn't. Definitely no. I wouldn't give any man at all a chance to start to get to know me, even; I can be pretty difficult to get to know, I'm very moody and taciturn and not usually very communicative, I keep myself to myself.

Beautiful things I liked I told you once didn't I; I couldn't stand ugliness or deformity. Philip was a very beautiful man, physically almost perfect, of perfect physique, as they say. So an Adonis, however good-looking, couldn't and wouldn't affect me now. You know, when I said I only liked beautiful things perhaps I should have been a little more precise, to make it perfectly clear. The emphasis is on the noun, not on the adjective. It's beautiful *things*, that's all.

*

CHAPTER TWO

ELEANOR KRAMER

*What I'm trying to say I guess is that somehow a man's there
and somehow a woman just isn't.*

Eleanor Kramer was American; the wedge of her high-cheek-
boned face was pinched and gaunt, with palely amber eyes
deep-set in it and close together, and her sandy hair was short
and cut in a severe straight fringe across her white forehead.
She never dressed in anything other than a faded maroon
woollen dress with a shapeless thick green cardigan over it,
with black woollen stockings and low-heeled brown canvas
shoes.

She was living in two fourth-floor rooms at the back of a
dilapidated house in a terrace near the end of a back street in
an overcrowded and dirty south London suburb. The accommodation was described and charged rent for as furnished:
one room was a small cell-like kitchen, and the other was
cramped with a wardrobe and a single bed along one wall, an
upright chair and a table with a typewriter on it against
another, and a cupboard, two trunks, a folded-up playpen and
some boxes against the third.

Threadbare and sunbleached dark green curtains were drawn
together at the window to exclude as much of the light of the
hot summer afternoons as possible. In a corner an arm-chair
sagged, losing its stuffing: near it was an oil-heater, lit and
with the wick turned up high, and in the middle of the room
was a drop-side cot, lined half way up the sides with foam-
rubber sheeting, and a blanket like a canopy stretched over the
top.

Eleanor sat on an upright dining-chair near it, with her arms
tightly folded, the whites of her knuckles showing the tightness
with which her hands gripped her elbows. She was thirty-
two.

—Sure I'm fine like this, please, you take the arm-chair, that's quite comfortable really. I'd much sooner sit here, I always do while he's asleep, then I can keep an eye on him and watch he's O.K. I've only just moved in here, I haven't gotten the room arranged properly yet, there's a problem with the furniture as you can imagine, to fix it so Joey can't hurt himself while he crawls around. So many corners and sharp edges; he's starting to get active now, it's gonna be even more of a problem soon. I'm glad I got all that extra foam-rubber sheeting over there in the corner, I'm gonna start putting it over all the danger points today, but it'll be a big job because there's so many of them. And under that bed there there's one of those, what do you call them, electricity power points; if he was to get his fingers to it it would be terrible, I'll have to try and fix it so one of the trunks is pulled across in front of it.

It's all very difficult you know, because each time you move the furniture around you don't always notice you've uncovered some new hazard he could hurt himself against, but I guess I've got enough of that rubber stuff to drape around to make everywhere safe.

I hope you're not too hot in here. Outside it's pretty warm I guess, but I'll maybe be taking him out to the shops later and it's very important for him always to have an even temperature I think, both inside and out of doors too. I put that blanket over the top of the cot to keep the light out so Joey can get his afternoon sleep properly, those curtains aren't too good. And the oil-heater's necessary because it gets too draughty in this room, the glass in the windows doesn't fit all that well. Yeah, sure, you go ahead and take off your jacket by all means; gladly, I don't mind, I'm not conventional or anything, please don't think that. Maybe we could talk kind of low could we, because otherwise Joey won't get his right amount of sleep, is that O.K.?

To start with, I guess it would help me very much if you were to ask me questions, yes: that would make things kind of much easier for me. Well I am thirty-two going on thirty-three, and I was born in Philadelphia. Most of my life I lived in Massachusetts in a small town just out of Boston. My father was an attorney: in England you would call that a lawyer I guess. Would you excuse me just a minute, I'll have a look see if Joey's all right—yes he's O.K.

Well my father and my mother, they were divorced when I
was young; I don't know how young exactly, I should say
maybe three or four, something like that. That was in Philadelphia, then he moved up to Boston with Audrey, that was
his second wife, my step-mother. They had three more children
so I have two half-sisters and one half-brother younger than
me; my half-brother is the eldest, he's maybe ten or eleven
years younger, that's quite a big gap. Oh hell, it sounds like
Joey's getting kind of restless, I wonder if he's all right; I wish
there was some way we could talk not so loud so it wouldn't
disturb him.

Sure we could move to the kitchen if you think that might be
better. Only I dunno, I don't think I could hear him so good
from there. Maybe we'd better go on like this a while. He
didn't sleep a lot last night, I thought he'd sleep all right this
afternoon, he ought to be tired, I know I certainly am. Well he
sounds O.K., he seems quiet again, if I sit like this with the
chair a bit closer to the cot I can watch him over the top.

Please don't think I'm not listening, I can hear perfectly
O.K. If you ask me some more questions I can hear fine, so
long as I don't make my voice too loud while I answer them.

My mother I remember virtually nothing about, no. She
didn't remarry, least not that I know of. That's right, yeah,
I've lost all contact with her, I've not seen or heard of her
since the divorce, I don't know what became of her. The
divorce, I don't know why it was: it just happened I guess. I
know she'd been in and out of mental hospitals most of her
life. Even when I was very young I think she must have been
because I don't remember her being around, I've no kind of
memory of her at all. I did hear once many years later she was
supposed to have been a schizophrenic, but that's considered
kind of a meaningless term these days, so I don't have any idea
what it was really. That's true, I do have a mental image of
her, yes. I don't know why it should be particularly, it's
probably very sentimental and romanticised, but I've always
thought maybe she was a kind of Blanche Du Bois, you know
like in 'A Streetcar Called Desire' of Tennessee Williams, that
sort of a person. Only because I know she'd been born in
Alabama, and someone told me once she was very ladylike and
sensitive; and she'd been a schoolteacher one time, she cared
about her appearance and I guess she put on airs about things,

and then she finally ended up bats. So I suppose that must have been something like she was, in a general sort of way.

I must have gotten most of that idea from the movie with Vivien Leigh, I saw it when I was about eighteen and I don't know why but I just kind of imagined that's maybe what she must have been like. No more than that, I've no other reason for saying it; except she was pretty once and then ended up like she did.

Are you O.K. Joey? He's breathing rather funny, sometimes he does that, he breathes with his mouth open but I guess he's all right, we can go on.

All of my childhood that I can recall I lived with Sam and Audrey, and we moved from near Boston when I was about nine and went to live in New York. That's right, Sam was my father, and Audrey was my step-mother. Yes I called them that right from when I can remember; in America, especially on the East Coast and in the cities where people are more sophisticated, it's quite usual for children to call their parents always by their Christian names. In England it's more of a socially smart thing isn't it, but it's quite ordinary in the States.

He's still got his mouth open, I don't know that he ought to do that, whether it's good for him. Oh good, he's closed it up again now, that looks more natural. He keeps opening his eyes and shutting them again though, like he's not too happy maybe at me talking so much. We shall have to keep our voices down lower still if we can.

Audrey was O.K. on the whole, I couldn't say I liked her a lot, but I don't think I hated her all that much either. I had the theory put to me once that if children dislike a step-parent very strongly all they're really doing is expressing in more socially-acceptable terms their feelings towards the true parent who isn't there any more. I wouldn't know if that was true in my case, because as I say I don't remember my mother at all except just the sound of scissors. On a table or the floor I mean, cutting out material to make maybe a dress or something for me. I think that must be why I still like that sound very much, it must remind me of her. It can't have been anything to do with Audrey because she never made clothes, there was no need; Sam was pretty comfortably off financially, so I didn't want for anything as a child.

The only other little thing about my mother was she took me

out some place and let me go without my galoshes on. She was like that, she was very indulgent. What that really showed was that she neglected me, I was told once: but I've never looked at it that way, I just think it was because she was very nice. But I don't think of Audrey as nice: I remember cursing her out once, I'd be eleven going on twelve around that time I suppose, and I'd been sent to my bedroom. I was shouting 'I bet she'll be making me wear these goddam leggings when I'm sixteen' which was the subject at issue we were rowing about. So I guess that shows she wasn't neglecting me doesn't it? I don't know, I've always been pretty messed-up and confused about the whole thing, and nobody's ever——

Oh can we stop just a minute, I think Joey's lying kind of funny, I ought to try to straighten him out. Yeah, he'll be more comfortable that way now, he should—oh goddam hell, look what I've gone and done now, I've woken him up. Did I disturb you honey? Honest, I was only trying to make you more comfortable that's all. No please don't cry. O.K., look, I'll tell you what, I'll lift you out, all right? You want to sit on the floor and play with your beaker toys? Do you want to play with your beakers? Look, they're here, you play with them. You don't want to play with them? See, watch, they go like this; this green one on top of this red one and then this blue one like that. You don't like them? O.K., if you don't want to do that you don't need to knock them around honey, just leave them, they won't hurt you. You do want them? I'll get them back for you, here. They're nice, look they're all different colours, that's right, you play with them.

No, it's O.K., we can still go on talking while he plays around. Here you are, you have this one as well Joey. . . . Well I guess it wasn't anything wrong with Audrey, in a way I just wished she wasn't there, that's all. You want a drink of water, Joey? Would you like for me to go get you a drink of water? I don't have any boiled-up, hell I should have done some ready and let it cool-off. I guess I ought to have thought of that. He still looks quite sleepy though. Would you like to go back in your cot again, do you want to go back to sleep again Joey? No O.K. you want to play with your beakers, well you play with your beakers if you want. What was I saying just now, yes Sam I was talking about, I was very fond of him. I still am too. I think I sort of hero-worshipped him as a little girl. Yeah well then we moved down to New York.

Joey, you don't want to play with your beakers anymore? O.K. then just leave them, you don't have to play with them if you don't want to. It was easier in New York because there was less scandal. Well, my father wasn't exactly a Communist but he had been examined at a Congressional hearing. I mean he was guilty, there was no doubt about that; he was definitely left-wing in his views, he never was a spy or anything but he thought that way politically. At that time if you admitted you did, well that was enough; people just didn't want to know you anymore. His practice went down and down so eventually we moved to New York so's he could get work and build it up again.

I think maybe Joey ought to have a drink of water or something, perhaps I'd better go boil some up for him.

*

The end of the road disintegrated into a wide patch of waste ground, rough-surfaced, dirty with litter and desolate. Once houses had been there, and presumably other buildings eventually would be; somewhere somebody probably had plans for something sometime. Meanwhile children used it for running about on, long-distance lorry drivers of firms which let them keep their vehicles near home parked them on the flat pieces, and owners of unwanted vans or cars left them there neglected and disconsolate to dissolve: they quickly disintegrated into plundered wrecks with no windows, wheels, engines, doors or seats.

As the evenings darkened the playing children went home. As they got darker still, street lamps came on, and old ladies in bedroom slippers brought small dogs out on leads for a last walk round the edge of the waste-patch before going to bed. When it was night a hunched bundle of rags which was a man could be caught sight of sometimes just before he squeezed inside the framework of one of the less-mutilated car skeletons and huddled down in its shelter.

Things were quiet then; everything was still, and it was time to put out the cigarette and go back up the street.

*

The kitchen had a stone sink with a cold-water tap under the uncurtained windows, and an old gas-cooker. There was a wall-cupboard, and beneath it a table with a canary yellow laminated top, and enough room at each end for a plain wooden chair.

—I guess it's kind of fortunate all you have to do to open the front door downstairs is push it. If the lock on it wasn't busted then I'd have to keep coming all the way down looking out for you, there's no bell or anything and none of the people on the ground floor'd bother to open it if you knocked. Everyone just keeps themselves to themselves in their own room all the time; even that telephone down there on the wall in the hall, no one'll answer it if it rings unless they happen to be passing it.

That makes things awkward for me; I can't help thinking I must have lost an awful lot of business these last few weeks. I certainly don't seem to be getting the response I thought I would to the ads I put in the papers. They cost money too, because they're in the good-quality national weeklies; if I don't get more response well it'll be a kind of a vicious circle, because then I shan't have any more money to go on putting them in. Well they just say 'Quick accurate professional typing at very reasonable rates', then my name and the number of that telephone down there. Only I can't hear it ringing from up here. The people on the ground floor, even when they do answer it all they say if someone asks for me is 'She's not in' and hang up again, because they can't be bothered coming right up here to see if I am.

I thought getting myself a place in a house with a telephone was going to be a great advantage business-wise, but it doesn't seem to be working out that way. I'll have to try and think of something else, some other way of organising the business so that at least it becomes economic. If I go on this way I shall have to sell the typewriter to keep on paying for the ads, which would be pretty ironic if you had that kind of a sense of humour which I guess I don't.

But I've got to get some work in somehow; I mean after all the hours of trouble I've taken to get the furniture arranged right so I could sit at a table and type, and yet at the same time keep Joey in sight in case he banged into something and hurt himself while he was crawling around on the floor. I've tried the playpen but he's taken against that somehow, he just screams all the time if I put him in it.

Leastways you coming this time every night is better, he's definitely asleep always by ten or ten-thirty or so, I don't have to worry so much about him. As long as you don't mind it means we have to sit out here in the kitchen always. And I think I think better at night too.

Would you mind passing me that newspaper parcel over so I can eat while we talk?

It's my supper. A piece of cabbage, chunk of bread, a piece of cheese. Actually it's my lunch, only I didn't finish it dinner-time because Joey was playing up. Sure I eat pretty good, I eat mainly fresh vegetables like this and carrots and things, I think they're best for you. Yesterday I had an egg, I think those are good for you too. I don't drink a lot of liquids, coffee or tea, stuff like that; mainly water. I guess I'll have some now with this: you like a glass of water too? Are you sure?

What sort of a day did I have today, well I guess it was just a kind of an ordinary one. No it wasn't either, it was kind of a good kind of a day because I did two things. One was I contributed a cleaning-cloth to the bathroom of this house down on the second floor. I left it there for anyone to use that wants to. Having done something like that is very important to me by way of establishing an independent life and identity of my own, it helps to give me good morale.

And the other thing I did was I made a 'phone-call. To something called 'Mothers in Action', have you ever heard of that? It's a sort of an organisation, I think, that represents single or unsupported mothers and tries to see they obtain their rights; more day nurseries, better financial provisions and so on, which I agree with one hundred percent. It also tries to get unsupported mothers to help each other, form local groups for mutual babysitting and that sort of thing. That was a very important thing I did today and it made me feel good that I'd done it. I got their 'phone-number months ago, I read it some-place, I've been carrying it around with me for months and never done anything about it, so that was a positive step that I took today to actually 'phone them. There was no reply from the number, so I guess there wasn't anybody there.

One other thing happened too. Joey's father came round,

and I asked him if he would baby-sit for me once or twice so I could go out and try and earn some money. This is the first time I've ever asked him anything of that kind, because I'd told him I'd never make any demands on him. I don't know whether it was right for me to ask him to do it or not. But my financial situation is getting very desperate now, so I felt I was forced to do it, to ask him I mean. Anyway he took it quite well I think, and he said he agreed he would. The trouble is he's not too reliable, so maybe I shouldn't build up my hopes very high about it. He also gave me a pound, which will help financially; I was rather surprised about it, that he should have the money I mean, because he doesn't have very much owing to his way of life, as a rule.

He's a busker, he plays guitar and sings on the street; so long as he gets enough money to live on for one day at a time he's happy to go along like that. I agree with him, I think that's how everybody should live. I don't see much of him these days, but I think he's a very nice person on the whole and I was pleased to see him.

So today has been a good day, because of all those things. Oh and another thing too was that some of the people in one of the rooms of this house, I think it might have been the one above this one, they had their record-player on: it was very loud and the music was nice, it made me feel happy to listen to. It was pop music with a sort of soul and blues sound to it, it made me happy to listen to it; kind of psychedelic it was, it made me wish I could have written music like that myself in the days when I used to compose.

Oh yes I can write music, or I could once. I have a degree in musical composition, I studied four years at university in America. I have a degree which is the equivalent of what is called Bachelor of Music here. Most of my composing, in fact all of it, was ten years or more ago now. Well it was string trios, quartets, settings of songs like Schubert's 'Die Schöne Müllerin', a song-cycle of the words of FitzGerald's Rubaiyat, stuff like that. I wasn't a great composer, I don't think the world's lost another Schonberg or anything. I'd like to think one day I'd start to write music again, but there are so many other things to get straightened out first; like my own life, how I'm going to earn my living, how to bring up Joey, even more immediate problems like where I'm to get money for next week's rent.

No, I don't go to the National Assistance Board. I never have. That would seem to me like the very end of the line, a sort of confession I couldn't manage my life anymore. I think it would be very bad for my morale indeed, it would probably destroy me as an individual person. So far I've managed to live two years on what money my husband gave me when we were divorced. He calculated it would last me one year until I could get on my feet, so I reckon I've done pretty good to make it last twice the time. Now there's just under £11 of it left; I don't reckon things can go on this way much longer. Least I didn't till Joey's father said today he'd baby-sit for me, so now I can go out and try and find work.

*

—I feel upset tonight, I don't mean I don't want to talk with you but I've sure had a couple of God-awful days yesterday and today.

You know how I told you I'd asked Joey's father if he'd do some baby-sitting for me while I went out and looked for some work? Well he came in the afternoon yesterday so I went around one or two agencies to see if they'd got any typing work I could bring back and do here, but they hadn't. And when I got back I found Joey's father had thought since it was a nice afternoon he'd take him to the park; he was letting him crawl around on the grass there, and he must have gotten onto the path or something, anyhow he tumbled over and scratched all his nose. I guess Roy must have been reading a book or looking at a newspaper or something. Whatever it was he wasn't watching Joey properly and so that's what happened. I was very upset about it when I got back, and called him a goddam fucking irresponsible pig and a few other things. I was so wild about it, and we had quite a row.

In fact I didn't think he'd offer to come anymore and baby-sit, but he did; I didn't ask him, he offered it himself, to come back again today. I didn't know if I ought to let him or not, but then I thought I ought to have one more try at getting work. I went out with my guitar in the Portobello Road, I stood on a corner and sang and played a few American and Russian folk-songs and things, and I did very well at it. I was only there about half-an-hour, and people were very generous; they threw money down on my jacket I'd put on the sidewalk in front of me, I got a total of somewhere around ten shillings or so.

But you know what had happened this time when I got back? That shitting idiot had let Joey bang himself on the table-leg; he's got a great big red bruise all down the side of his face here. Jesus, what with that and the skin scraped off his nose he looks terrible, he looks like he's been in a war or something. I threw him out, Joey's father I mean; I'm sure not gonna let him anywhere near Joey again, he's got no idea how to look after a child. I mean I couldn't go out to work anytime and leave him with him, I'd be so scared something'd happen, he'd have another accident.

I'm sorry to be so jumpy all the time, I do, I feel awful, all this has really upset me terribly. I'll tell you what, I'll just go have another look at him, make sure he's sound asleep, not showing any signs of brain damage or anything. If he's O.K. we can settle down and I can tell you more of my life story, I guess it might help me to think about something else for a while. I'll go check Joey's O.K., will you excuse me a minute? You want a drink of water, if you do go ahead help yourself from the tap, it's quite good the water round here, there's maybe a beaker or something in the sink to drink it out of. I'll just stay in there a minute and listen to him, make sure he's all right and then I'll be right back.

Three minutes. Silence. From the tap single drops of water fell at ten second intervals into an unwashed pan in the sink. Five minutes. Silence. Single drops of water fell at ten second intervals into the unwashed pan in the sink. Seven minutes. Silence. Far away a dog barked three times. Drops of water splashed into the pan. Ten minutes. Splash. Splosh. Splash. Splosh.

—As far as I can tell he sounds O.K., you can't really properly estimate it if you only listen a minute or two like that, but I didn't want to keep you waiting. It must be nearly midnight now I guess, perhaps he'll sleep through now. I'll leave this door open just a little so I can hear if he does make any sort of a noise like if he's in pain or anything. He's been fine this evening while he was awake, took his mashed potato and gravy and custard and fruit and stuff for his supper, had a good crawl around and played with his beakers after, he looked O.K. that far. He went to sleep around ten, that's when you can't really tell anymore, know what I mean; his eyes aren't open, he's not moving anymore, so you don't exactly know what's going on, I mean he might be O.K. but then on the other hand he might not.

Anyhow I'll go on with my life story, we'll see how far we get. Like I said it'll give me something else to think about. Did you have any water? You sure you don't want some?

I lived in New York with Sam and Audrey like I told you, and we had a nice apartment. Sam was a good lawyer, he'd soon gotten his practice up again, people were more tolerant in New York, they weren't expecting to find a Commie under every bed like they had been up in Boston.

I took my degree in music when I was 20, I'd moved on from school to university then. And as soon as I got the degree I got married. My husband was quite a nice sort of a guy, but it wasn't a marriage for love or anything, more what you might call a marriage of convenience. I wanted to get away from home because I didn't like living with Audrey and the kids who were so much younger than me. Vincent, that was the man I married, well I guess he just wanted himself a wife: he was a mathematics tutor at university. I think scientifically minded people, they very often do marry what might be called artistic type people, to kind of round-out their lives.

Oh no, we weren't in love with each other at all, it was just almost more or less a straight business deal. I even forget how we met now, it might have been at some mutual friends' house maybe, something like that. We met a few times more after that, we had a few talks, I told him what I wanted and he told me what I wanted, and they seemed to kind of fit together and so that was that. He wanted a fairly presentable sort of wife who was a bit artistic, to help him along with his career in the academic world, and I wanted to get away from home and improve my economic and social status; so it seemed a good idea.

Well you know how it is in the States; or maybe you don't know how it is. You don't, well O.K. I'll try and explain it to you. There's a lot of this thing over there: kids whose fathers are earning say thirty thousand dollars a year get to be juvenile delinquents because they feel deprived in comparison with other kids whose fathers are earning fifty thousand dollars a year. I'm not saying Sam my father was poverty-stricken exactly, but he had been knocked back because of having to move from where we lived near Boston. He certainly wasn't earning the same kind of money Vincent was, nor were his prospects anything like so good. He was a much older man naturally, and he had a wife and two kids to support. Whereas Vincent was just starting out on what was going to be a very fine career. And equally he was respectable, and Sam wasn't; and respectability was something I very much wanted.

My father wasn't respectable because of that thing I told you about, that he had actually been questioned at a Congressional hearing; you've no idea what that meant over there in those days. They had nothing on him like spying, but once something like that had happened to you, you had to live very quietly; it was a shameful thing you had to cover up all the time, especially if you were a professional man like my father was. I wanted to get away from all that, I wanted to get right away and become a decent citizen again. I had my music degree, and that gave me some standing but not very much, not enough. So that's what I meant by improving my social as well as my economic status. It seemed a very good idea, only it didn't work out.

I wasn't a very stable character I guess, I'd been having this mental trouble, depressions when I used to lie on my bed the whole day and not move, just stare up at the ceiling, and I thought getting married might cure that but it didn't. Also more or less exactly around the same time, within six months of the marriage or even less maybe, I met Michael and fell in love with him and we were having this very passionate affair; and in between times I was having depressions and psychotherapy and all that stuff, so the whole thing was just one hell of a big mess all round.

Then naturally I suppose, one day Vincent told me he was sorry but he couldn't go on with it, we'd had a business deal but as far as he was concerned it was through, he wanted to dissolve the partnership. That was all right by me; I could see myself it'd been a mistake by the both of us. We arranged he should divorce me on the grounds of my continuing adultery with Michael with whom I was living nearly all the time then anyway. The legalities took a while to fix but eventually the marriage was officially ended by the court; it had lasted four years more or less to the week I think.

I was worried a bit then because I was very much in love with Michael and I wasn't sure if he was with me. I wondered how I was going to make out. But he said he really and truly was in love with me and he would like it if we got married, so we did; the only condition he laid down was that I should go on with having treatment under a psychiatrist.

That worked out well for a time, Michael started having psychiatric treatment too. But we were moving around a lot, he was a construction engineer, the company he worked for had a lot of Government contract work. We lived in Pittsburgh, Baltimore, Richmond, Detroit, all over the place; a few months here, a year there, six months somewhere else. We were pretty happy I guess; well fairly happy most of the time; or quite a lot of the time anyway. Except for me, I wasn't all that happy at all, because I didn't seem to be anybody, I didn't have any kind of personality of my own. And instead of me getting nearer finding one it seemed like I was moving further away from it all the time. We definitely didn't want to have children, because I didn't feel I could until I'd become a mature sort of person and gotten myself a bit more sorted out.

Then after three years Michael's company offered him a job over here in England, they were starting building plant and factories and things in Europe; it was going to be a top job developing one of their subsidiaries. We decided it would be a very good thing to do, to leave the States and make a kind of a fresh start altogether over here. It seemed a good thing from my point of view too; I looked upon it as an opportunity to revitalise our marriage which wasn't turning out too good, and for me to rebuild my own personality again. So that's what we did, we came over here to make this fresh start. Only it didn't work out.

We'd been here only a few months and then I met Roy, and I started sleeping with him, sometimes I stayed with him a week or more without letting Michael know where I was. I don't think I was in love with Roy, but I found him physically attractive and I liked his way of life. It seemed to me good to live the way he did, and not worry much about money and possessions and things, not kind of belong anywhere or to anybody but just be a pure individual and belong to yourself. By that time I wasn't in love with Michael any more, I liked him very much and I still do like him now; but I didn't love him in the sense of wanting to be with him all the time, I thought a lot of his values were wrong. He definitely wasn't in love with me by then either, and I don't know how things would have turned out, I guess we'd have gone along until something happened. In fact that's how it was, something did happen: Michael met this English girl, I don't know her name or anything about her, but he told me one day that he'd met her and wanted to marry her.

I thought it would only be fair to him to allow that to happen, because probably she would be more compatible for him. So he divorced me on the grounds of my adultery with Roy, and now he's gotten married to her. He was very generous to me, he said he knew I would have a hard time until I got work and got on my feet, so he gave me a sum of money sufficient for me to live on for a year. Only like I said, by being very careful I've made it last two years, which I feel proud of having done.

When the divorce was through I was in a bit of a state then, I was thirty years old, going on thirty-one, and I thought for Christ's sake what in hell have I got to show for my life, absolutely nothing of my own at all. So I 'phoned up Michael where he was working, I asked him could we meet for a coffee because there was something I wanted to ask him. When we met I said now that the divorce was all final and everything, would he give me a baby so I could at least have something, but he said no.

So then I asked Roy, I told him I wouldn't make any demands on him for it, which was a pretty damn fool thing for me to say I guess, because of the financial aspect I mean. In the end he said well if I promised then O.K. he would, and he did: we had to try only a couple of times and I got pregnant. And that's how it happened that things are this way now. I thought having a baby might change me, help me get back some kind of identity of my own. Only so far it hasn't worked out.

Joey was a year old a week ago last Tuesday, and I guess things have got to change pretty soon now, or I've got to work out some way of making them change. Even just from the financial point of view, in two weeks time I'll have no money left at all and——

Oh my gosh, I wonder if he's all right. He hasn't made a sound or anything all this time, I haven't been listening out properly because I've been talking, if you don't mind we shall have to stop now, I really ought to be paying more attention to his condition, not just sitting here so long talking about myself, that's terrible.

*

At no time was there ever, or could be, any continuity of conversation or concentration. Over the weeks, questions had to be repeated again and again; the answers to them came in spurts and stops and starts and fragments and rephrasings and recapitulations. These are some of the questions, with the answers to them put together from sentences and phrases dispersed like fallen wind-swirling leaves: arranged into consecutive order and coherence, though they were never spoken so.

What psychiatric treatment have you had and how helpful has it been?

—I must have had every kind that there is nearly, over a period of ten or maybe twelve years.

Back in the States psychoanalysis is very fashionable, especially on the East Coast and in the cities. Everybody talks about 'my analyst says this', and 'my therapist says that'; sometimes you get the impression you can't take part in any kind of social conversation at all unless you are having treatment or have had it. I think a lot of it is what Eric Fromm calls a search for a magical helper; I know it was so in my case, especially in my late teens and early twenties before and after I got married, both times.

All in all I should say I went to six, maybe seven different psychiatrists and therapists: the longest was for just over two years, the shortest two or three months. Sometimes the break was because that particular person treating me moved away to another job, sometimes it was because I moved to live in a different place when my husband's job made it necessary, and sometimes I broke off treatment myself, because I felt it wasn't getting me any place and was simply a waste of money. They say if you do that it's because you're too scared to go on, but I don't think it was in my case: it was honestly and truly because I felt it was doing me no good at all. It wasn't even upsetting me, or making any kind of impression or change, which is what it's supposed to do I guess; upset you I mean, shake you up and make you look at yourself.

It certainly was, and still is, very expensive indeed to have analysis or therapy in the States. I think the lowest I was ever charged was about seven dollars for a session of 40 minutes, and the most I paid—or more correctly my father or my husband paid—was maybe fifteen or twenty dollars a session. It'd take me some time to work it out, but I could do that for you. Yes, I've worked it out, it would have been in total something well over two thousand dollars in all; that would be more than one thousand pounds in your currency. That's what the psychiatric treatment I have had has cost altogether.

Whether it did me any good or not is very difficult to answer. Sometimes I think yes it did at the particular time, if I was very depressed or unsettled, it calmed me down to have somebody to go and talk to. Often when you were in a bad emotional state the thought that a day or two days later you'd be able to talk about it to somebody was a help in stopping you doing other things, maybe something of a more violent nature to yourself or somebody else. But it never made any fundamental change in me, or helped me feel more definite as a person in my own right. I read some of the books by a psychiatrist called Dr. R. D. Laing since I came over here: somebody told me his ideas were very good, and I think maybe they are. But my trouble is I can't follow them, they're much too metaphysical for me, they get me more fogged than ever. Not that I think reading books is much use for anyone anyway, really. I only ever read one thing in a book that I thought was any good; it was a sentence in a novel of Dostoevsky's. What was it now, oh yes: 'Better an active melancholy than an inactive despair.'

Another thing about analysts and therapists that puts me off them is the way they go about things. They're always trying to get you to break down in the session with them, and if you don't do that they feel they're not getting any place. This seems to me all wrong. They tell me to think about my mother and my feelings about her, to let out the latent hostility towards her which they say I'm bottling up inside me. I say to them that as far as I know I don't have such feelings, but I'll go away and think about them, and then come back and talk. That never seems good enough for them; they want you to do it there and then, maybe shout and swear and burst into tears in front of them in their consulting-room or whatever. If I was going to do that I'd sooner do it in private, and then tell them about it afterwards. But they try and provoke you into doing it while you're with them. I find this very objectionable, to me it seems almost like a kind of mental housebreaking on their part, an intrusion into my privacy which I haven't invited.

I've also had other forms of treatment with different anti-depressant drugs of one kind or another. Most of them have been good, at least as far as the immediate problem was concerned; they've always made me feel much less depressed while I was taking them. You get a sort of mental kick from them. If I was to get bad feelings of depression now any time, I'd go to a doctor and ask him to prescribe something of that kind for me.

Since I've come to England I've felt that way twice. The first time was not long after we'd been here: I didn't want to ask my husband for money for private treatment because he'd spent so much on it already, so I went to a doctor and asked him if he could get me an appointment to see somebody at a hospital. This took months to arrange, and when I did finally get to see the hospital doctor and we talked things over, he said the only kind of treatment he gave was therapy and as far as he could see there would be no point in my case because he considered I was too resistant to the idea for it to be of help to me. The other time was when I was pregnant with Joey and I got to feeling very depressed. That time I asked another doctor to prescribe me some pills. He was going to, but when I told him I was pregnant he said in that case it wouldn't be safe for me to take them, so he didn't give me anything at all. Anyway, after a while the depression went away of its own accord.

In the year since Joey was born I have felt it was coming back maybe a couple of times. I've thought of going to a doctor but so far I haven't. On the whole I don't want to go to one ever again anyway; I get to feeling very guilty and shameful about the whole thing, this having to ask other people's help the whole time, I feel this is wrong and I must do it myself. I mean for Christ's sake I'm a grown-up woman, not a kid anymore, I'll never learn to be mentally self-supporting if I go on like this.

Whose help would you take?
—What, economically or mentally, do you mean? Economically so far I've been taking the help of my ex-husband from that money he gave me but that's more or less run out now: once or twice these last few weeks Joey's father's given me a few shillings or a pound on one occasion. I've never requested money from him because that was the agreement we had when I asked him for the baby. It's always been money he's given to me now and again, I suppose just when he had it in his pocket. He's not the sort of person who ever has much, or needs it or thinks other people should. I agree with that, I think it's wrong that money should be so important that you have to have it just to keep on living, and I wouldn't ever ask him for any.

And I certainly wouldn't go and apply for something which I think is called National Assistance here, which is public money they give you after they've assessed exactly how great your need for it is. It seems to me entirely wrong someone should work out how much money another person is in need of, and then give it to them. I think it would be very demeaning indeed, it would degrade me very much as a person and an individual.

I wouldn't accept charity from anybody, either for myself or for Joey. I believe there are certain charities which exist for women with babies who are not married: the main one is something called The National Council for the Unmarried Mother and Her Child. I would certainly never have anything to do with that, because I think it's a terrible thing that it should even exist. I saw a poster of theirs once, it was a picture of a little boy and it said 'Illegitimate? That's His Hard Luck.' I think that was a very wicked thing indeed, because it would implant in the mind of everybody who saw it the idea that illegitimacy is a misfortune which a child has to bear all through life. Maybe in some senses it is, but it seems to me posters like that only help everyone think it really and truly is something to be ashamed of, and feel pity towards others for it if they are. Pity is a horrible thing to have people feel about you or your child; and additionally to anyone who is grown-up and illegitimate themselves, and already feeling in some kind of way ashamed about it like a lot of illegitimate people do, the poster would be most offensive to them too, I should think.

Also I don't know if you've ever seen the names of the people connected with the National Council for the Unmarried Mother. Most of them are titled people of the do-gooder kind, who want other people to know about the good work they think they are doing, and therefore they have their names printed on appeals-leaflets and annual reports and so on. No, I'm not saying this because it's just an impression I've got out of nowhere: I've had dealings with them myself in the past, and everything that happened confirmed my bad impression of them.

Well I 'phoned them up one day to ask if they had lists of accommodation for single mothers with babies. They told me they didn't give out information on the 'phone, I would have to call and see them. A few days later I went right over the other side of London with Joey to get there, and when I did and asked could I see their accommodation-list, then they said I couldn't, I would have to make a proper appointment to go back and see them. I was pretty damn furious, but since I was there already I said O.K. I'd do that and I did, and they gave me an appointment for a few days later.

That meant another trail right over there on 'buses and tubes and things carrying Joey all the way; this time they'd given me an appointment all right but they told me it was to see a social worker. All I wanted was a list of accommodation so I could try and find somewhere to live; they hadn't even asked me did I want to see a social worker in the first place, I was just so disgusted I walked right out again. Their whole organisation, their name and everything, it implies the first thing you've got to do is go and confess yourself in a low-status position, as someone who's mismanaged her affairs and needs the help of social workers and wealthy do-gooding ladies.

I guess the real trouble is their organisation's masculine-orientated like the rest of society; they're on the defensive, trying to defend women, who they agree are poor unfortunate second-class human beings. I reckon they're conniving at that whole kind of attitude and what's worse helping to perpetuate it, by calling themselves what they do and presenting their work to the public in that fashion.

Yes we do live in a masculine-orientated society, there's no getting away from that at all; but there's no rule saying you have to like it. You'd have to be a woman to understand properly just how it is and what it means.

What's it like to be a woman?
—It's just like kind of well pretty goddam awful, I'd say, I guess. Maybe if you were a Negro you'd understand, or a Jewish person, but otherwise no man could understand it at all ever; it's a foreign country, and if you're not a native of it you can't really know what it's like because you don't live in that land.

What I'm trying to say I guess is that somehow a man's there and somehow a woman just isn't. A man has a personality, he has rights and privileges simply by virtue of him being a man and no more than that. Things like a man can get his wife written off as a tax-allowance on a form, like all his other expenses, his house-mortgage, his insurance, his travelling-costs for whatever business he's in and all the rest of it.

It's because of the way society is based economically; the whole set-up diminishes women as individuals. Like in my own case for instance, if I want to live and have children I've got to do it under the financial protection of a man; I have to marry him or live with him and let him look after me, I can't do it by myself on my own. I have to sort of sell my personality to his, in exchange for him giving me the money to feed and clothe the children, and naturally this keeps me in an inferior position to him all the time. The basic economics of the situation force you into a personal relationship with someone, whether you want to or not. And if the personal relationship breaks down and you're the woman then you're right up against it because you've been so dependent on him up till then: not only financially but also emotionally as well, even if it meant no more than him having the right to decide whether or not to go on putting up with you.

And once he makes up his mind he doesn't want to do that anymore, you're out on your own. You don't dare not put up with him, or at least you let him push you a lot further down along the line and you go on putting up with him, because you know the moment you break apart you're going to be the one who feels the loneliness: much more you because you're a woman and your resources and recourses are much less than his. I mean you hear how husbands have rows with their wives and they go off and get drunk to relieve their feelings, and then they go back again. But what does a woman do when she has a row with her husband? She can't go and do that, she has to scream or break saucers or something, and as soon as she does she gets called hysterical or some other derogatory name.

You're conditioned into this right up from childhood, men are big and strong and clever, women are small and weak and stupid. They're the bosses, the ones who make the decisions and all the running. They can have affaires easier, they can do most anything they like. and no one blames them for it so long as they get away with it. But if you're a woman you can't just call a guy up on the telephone, and say you feel like a bit of sex, and will he come round and give it you. If you did you'd be called a nymphomaniac, which is a derogatory word used to describe women only; there's no equivalent word can be applied to a man. And not just sex, almost everything else: if it's only a drink you want, if you go some place by yourself people look at you just because you're a woman doing it on her own and the correct thing to do is to get a man to take you.

And as for if you've got feelings for a man, emotional feelings which you could call love perhaps, then you're really on the hook; you're all the time thinking about his feelings, are they the same as yours, is he going to call you up, is he going to come and see you like he promised, if he doesn't does it mean he doesn't like you any more, what is it you've done wrong that's upset him, what have you said, have you lost him?

I don't think men feel that way about women, I don't think many of them get into that sort of tangle; or if they do they don't show it. They either go right out to get what they want, or if they can't have it they go and do something else instead to take their minds off it. A woman can't do that: there aren't all that many things a woman can do on her own initiative: she just has to sit there and feel inadequate at her own power-lessness, which she can't ever do anything about because that's the way she's constituted, that's what she is, she's a woman.

And that doesn't mean I wish I was a man or anything: what it means is I wish women weren't like women are. I don't think they were made properly, there was a fault back in the planning stage somewhere. That's why I'm sure glad Joey's a boy, I think life's gonna be much easier for him because he doesn't have to go through it with the handicap of being female; he won't have the burden of worries to carry around with him like I always have.

What are your worries?

—I don't have any big ones really, not a lot apart from the financial aspect of things which is the main one at the moment, and my trouble with my personal morale. I'd say only the daily superstitions I have, which get me down sometimes because they waste so much time. I don't know what to do about them because they're ridiculous, but anyway everyone has those.

No I don't mean black cats or walking under ladders or anything silly of that sort; I think all that stuff's crazy, I don't believe in any of it, how could anyone? It's the purely personal thing, everybody has it. Oh you know what I mean, this walking around tidying things up which I do and trying to make sure it's in the right order. It gets so difficult sometimes to make sure it's right and I don't make any mistakes about it.

Well I'm sure you do know how I mean, after all it's the same for everyone. The order you pick things up in.

You know, should I move this chair first, then draw the curtains, then fold up those blankets of Joey's, then wind the clock—or should I wind the clock first, then fold the blankets, and leave drawing the curtains and moving the chair to the last. Or should it be the blankets first, then the curtains, followed by winding the clock and moving the chair. It takes goddam ages to work it out sometimes. It's very important you should get it right because if you don't something awful will happen. Well I don't know like what do I, until whatever it is that it's going to be actually happens. That's why I'm so particular to get the order right in the first place so it won't happen. I have to rely on intuition largely, sometimes it gets pretty exhausting, it takes me maybe half an hour to work it out before I feel confident enough to start off the sequence. But that's rather trivial and ordinary anyway.

No I couldn't say I've any really big worries at all. I mean I never read newspapers or anything, so I'm not worried about what goes on in the outside world, wars and things. I can't do anything about them, they've nothing to do with me, it would be foolish of me to use up my mental energies worrying about things of that kind.

I don't worry about cosmic things, God and all that kind of stuff. I don't believe there is a God, or that nature all fits together beautifully; it's just a bungle as far as I can see, and I don't think about it or worry about it, because to do that would be a waste of time also.

So important worries, no I don't really have any great ones at all, nor many particular little ones either. I wouldn't describe myself as being a very worrying sort of person by nature.

Joey? Sure I worry about him a bit sometimes, I mean what mother doesn't about her child? How he's going to grow up, what sort of person he's going to be, that sort of thing. But not a lot. Just so's he doesn't hurt himself by banging into the furniture or things falling on him, or getting some kind of illness. But not a lot.

Sometimes I think I ought to worry more about him than I do, in case somebody thought I wasn't concerned for him like a mother ought to be. But then when I do it seems to cause a lot of bad feeling very often. Well like with doctors and people, I mean; that's why I have to keep changing from one to another because they all get so unpleasant.

I think it's only natural if you've got something not quite right with your baby you want to know if it's serious or not; but most doctors I've come across so far don't seem to me all that responsible in their attitudes. Joey's very susceptible to things, he's always getting colds or a funny little cough he has every once in a while, or he gets very pale looking sometimes, or hot looking, or he doesn't get enough sleep, or sometimes he sleeps far too long for what I think a baby should.

Most doctors seem all the same, I mean at first they're usually O.K. but then they start getting uptight after a while. This one I'm registered with now at the moment, I guess I'll have to change to someone else pretty soon if he goes on like he is. He won't even make house-calls any more, he was quite offensive that I should call him in three times in one week. The last time all I'd wanted was his opinion did he think that playpen was safe, and I can't see what was so terrible about that. It's a very important thing to know, it didn't look to me I was wasting his time like he said, I don't see how he could advise me unless he actually saw it.

He's even started getting angry now when I just call him up on the 'phone to tell him how Joey's looking and ask him if it's normal. I have to call him up because when I used to take Joey to his surgery he got madder with me every time and told me to think about the other people he'd got waiting outside to see him. All I'd ever wanted him to tell me was whether he thought the way Joey looked pale was anything to worry about, or if it was just an ordinary cough he'd got, and things like that. I don't dare take him in to see him anyway this week, he looks so awful with that scratch and that bruise he's got, I guess he might even start thinking I'd been mistreating him or something.

So that's another thing I'll have to do I guess, change my doctor again. But they do all seem to be the same around here, or the five I've had so far do.

Well sure I get a bit angry with Joey sometimes if he gets into mischief, but that's all. I mean if he crawls around and disturbs my furniture arrangement which I've gone to all the trouble to work out for his own safety. And sometimes I resent a bit the loss of freedom which having him entails, there are certain things I could do if I hadn't got him. But not a lot, I don't feel like that a lot. I don't resent having him, I mean that would be just too terrible altogether; no mother could or should think that, ever, it would be too awful even to think about it.

Well I guess I have sworn at him occasionally when my feelings have got the better of me. Just the other night I screamed and screamed at him maybe ten minutes or quarter of an hour without stopping, I should think. Oh I cursed him and damned him, and I called him a bastard too, and I meant it. I told him he was terrible and goddam awful and dreadful and all that, and I shook him real hard and chucked him down in his cot and that made him cry all the more. It was all real noisy with the row the two of us were making, I was surprised nobody complained from one of the other rooms but they didn't. But I don't do that kind of thing very often, not a lot. He'll be a baby for a long time yet, I get very kind of fatalistic and indifferent about it sometimes because there is nothing I can do to alter the situation.

Do you ever read in books or newspaper reports about people who kill children? Sometimes when I go in the library and I happen to see something like that, it's kind of strange you know; I just always have to read cases of that sort right the way through from beginning to end, maybe twice even, they have a sort of morbid fascination for me. I read all the details, I can't seem to drag myself away from them.

But on the whole I'd say no, I have no worries really.

This is the last night I shall see you: what will happen to you from now on?

—I guess I don't know.

*

CHAPTER THREE

ANN KENT

I'm afraid I'm not the sort of person who talks very easily about things like love.

—Right on the dot eh? Good for you, nice to see you, come in, let's take your coat, sit yourself down then. Kettle's on ready and boiling, nice cup of tea after your drive? How's the traffic out of town tonight, not too bad? Jack's gone out for the evening to the Bingo. What? Sorry, you'll have to shout, can't hear you out here in the kitchen, I'm laying the tray. Got some ginger biscuits tonight on the way home; like those all right, do you?

Right, here we are then, I'll just let the tea brew a minute or two. You're looking tired tonight; had a hard day have you? Mustn't overdo it now; if you don't feel up to coming any time, just give me a tinkle on the 'phone, you know, we can always make it another night instead. I mean it's not as if I ever go out anywhere, I'm always free in the evenings.

Bone china cups and saucers, red with gold rims on a tray with a freshly ironed white cloth; a plate of biscuits, the gleaming aluminium tea-pot, the cut glass milk-jug and sugar bowl. Ann Kent placed it on a stool where she could easily reach it, took the lid off the tea-pot to give the contents a brisk stir, flipped open a packet of cigarettes, lit one, kicked off her shoes and curled up comfortably with her feet tucked underneath her in an armchair. Levelly and straight, she smiled, and with one hand smoothed down the hemline of her plain blue woollen skirt across her knees, while the other briefly checked the fastenings of the buttons on her crisp white high-collared blouse. Short and closely cut, her helmet of dark curly hair, and bright coffee-brown eyes. A neat figure, compact, every movement precise; pretty, confident, at ease in the sitting-room of the comfortably furnished council flat. She had been born there, and had lived in it all of her life's twenty-seven years.

—Before, I thought I might be scared you know; funny isn't it, how you get used to the idea of talking about yourself after a while? Never done a lot of that in our family, not great ones for talking about ourselves. Plenty of laughs and jokes, just an occasional serious remark now and again, that's about all. Pity, really: there's been times often when I'd like to have said things and haven't; and then I've regretted it afterwards, know what I mean? Specially when you realise you're never going to get the chance to, no more.

My Mum particularly, I was thinking of; there's lots of things now I wish I'd said to her while she was alive. It's struck me more and more since she died two years ago; I've felt, you know, there were things I did really ought to have said. To thank her, chiefly; let her know how much I appreciated all she did for me, tell her how good she'd been to put up with me. When she was dying, she was laying there in hospital, a good few weeks it went on; we knew there was no hope. Me and one of my sisters used to go in alternate nights and sit with her; the hospital were very good, they let us stay as long as we wanted. Of course there was nothing we could do, she was unconscious all the time; but that was when I first felt it, I thought I'd like to say things to her then, but it was too late, there was no chance.

Shirley, that's my sister, she and her husband when I told them about it afterwards they said there was no need to worry; they said Mum would have known. It does just sort of niggle at me still though, that I ought to have done, and I didn't.

I was, well I was so ashamed you see. But I never got the chance to tell her just how ashamed, how sorry I was for all the trouble and worry I'd caused through what I'd done.

*

—Yes, I liked being a kid. It was the happiest time of my life. They always say it is, don't they; but you never realise it at the time. I don't mean I've got unhappy as I've become older, because I haven't. I'd say I was happy most of my life more or less, apart from the odd moment now and again; but we all get those, don't we? The unhappiest moment of my life ever? Oh I'd say when Mum died, I don't think there's no question of that. When we all came back here to the flat after the funeral; everybody talking, and it suddenly came home to me, I was never going to see her again, never again, sitting in that chair you're in now which was her favourite one. She wasn't going to come in through that door no more, she wasn't going to be out there in the kitchen getting supper ready when I got in from work. I suppose it must have struck my brother Jack too, just the same: from now on there was only going to be the three of us, him and me and my Mary. My other two sisters, Shirley and Pam, it wasn't so bad for them because they were married, they'd got husbands and children of their own and homes to go back to. But Jack and I, we hadn't.

Still, I'd got Mary, which was more than Jack had: so I shouldn't feel too sorry for myself, should I, not compared with him? He's got no one, and nothing at all. Anyway that's nothing to do with it really, has it; you said which was my unhappiest moment. So I'd say that was it; the day of the funeral, coming back here and realising Mum was gone. It was only a couple of years ago you know, but it still makes me feel very sad to think about it.

It was much worse than when Dad died. Which'd be what, nine, ten years ago now. I was sad then too, but nothing like in the same way. I liked him well enough, but I wasn't as close to him, I never had been. He went very sudden, had a heart attack, over before you knew it had happened almost, know what I mean? Terrible shock, but somehow you do adjust to it; you get over it quite quickly, or at least I did, it's surprising. Course Mum was very upset, but I think I spent more time thinking about trying to cheer her up than feeling sorry myself, and I suppose it was doing that that helped me. It does, doesn't it, when you've got to think about somebody else before yourself.

And then again with Mum there'd been this long period beforehand, the weeks she was in hospital when we knew she was dying and they'd told us there was no hope for her. In a way that made it worse, because you can't help hoping, can you? Even though they'd told us it was coming, it didn't make it any better, or any easier to get over it when it happened. Yes, it was all very sad was that: and the saddest part of all was coming back here afterwards, definitely.

The happiest moment of my life? Oh that's easy, I can remember that without even hardly having to think about it. It was when my Mary was about six months old, I should think she'd be. I'd bathed her and fed her and changed her nappy, and I'd left her lying on the bed there in my room. My sister Shirley was here for the evening and she was in the room with me, I asked her would she keep an eye on Mary for a minute while I went back to the bathroom to get something: I don't remember what it was, powder or a nightgown or something. It doesn't matter, anyway I couldn't find it; I was looking round everywhere, it took me five minutes at least before I went back in the bedroom again.

Shirley didn't know I was back there, she hadn't heard me come in. She was lying on the edge of the bed, with Mary between her and the wall. Not doing anything; just looking at her, watching her lifting her feet up and her hands, wriggling them about in the air, gurgling a bit and making little sort of happy noises to herself.

You know, I just stood by the door and looked at them without making a sound, till Shirley realised I was there and moved off the edge of the bed to let me pick Mary up and put her down in her cot. Shirley'd already got two kids of her own; I don't know why, but I felt so proud she was happy just to lie like that and look at mine, with such an expression of pleasure and enjoyment all over her face. Silly, isn't it? I got a terrific feeling at that moment, of pure happiness. I can't explain it; but I haven't, I've never felt anything like it, either before or since.

So for the moment of happiness, there's no question of it either, that was the biggest one I've ever had. Would you like another biscuit? Go on, do, I got them specially for you coming. That's right; pass your cup, there's plenty more tea in the pot. Help yourself to sugar; there you are.

Well I suppose you'll have to get it into some sort of order, my life, won't you? You shouldn't let me go rambling on; I will, I'll talk your head off now I've got used to it. What sort of order do you think would be best, my life story right through from the beginning up to the present day? All right then, if you think you can stand it. I ought to warn you though, it's not a very interesting one. I'm just an ordinary girl, an ordinary unmarried mother, and that's about it. Well if you say so, yes all right that's how I'll do it; I'll tell you the whole story as I see it and then leave it to you.

Could you just give me a bit of a start though; will you, you know what I mean, ask me something to get me going? Yes: right, good, off we go then.

The very very first thing I remember is a lovely teddy-bear I had that was called a 'Hug-Me' teddy, because I think that was the name of the manufacturers. She was all soft and cuddly and nut brown; she had big ears and black glass eyes, and she made a growling noise if you bent her over and then sat her up again. She was really smashing, she was. Oh I just called her 'Hug-Me', because that was her name. A teddy called 'Hug-Me'; that's the first thing I remember, I can still see her now. I've no idea what became of her; I think perhaps when I got too old for her Mum put her away, then perhaps she gave her to Shirley for one of her children. Or perhaps she gave her to Pam, that's my other sister, when she and her husband had their first little boy. I don't know what happened to her at all, really I'd have to ask them if they know. 'Whatever became of "Hug-Me"?' They'd think I'd gone potty, wouldn't they?

Well, our family was Mum and Dad, and they had four children. Jack was the eldest, then there was Pam, then there was Shirley, and last there was me. Jack's thirty-three now, and Pam's thirty-one, Shirley's twenty-nine and I'm twenty-seven; we were all nicely spaced out at two year intervals, weren't we? My father was a milk roundsman, then I think he was a dustman; then he went in the army for the war, and after he came out he went on the 'buses as a driver, and he stayed doing that for the rest of his life until he died. He was never a man who could have settled to an indoor job in an office or anything of that sort, he always preferred being out and about. I think a man's man is what I could best describe him as, really. He liked an active life; in fact to be quite honest sometimes I think he used to overdo it. I mean he wasn't much of a family man. He'd never go out shopping with Mum, or things like that. I remember telling him once there was a picture on at the local cinema she wanted to see; and all he did was he gave me ten bob and said 'Here you are then, you take her.'

He wasn't cruel, they weren't unhappy, nothing of that sort.

Just that he preferred being on his own most of the time I suppose. He got a bit better towards the end of his life, I think; the last five or six years of it he did seem to spend more time in her company. He'd go out with her occasionally, say if they were choosing a new carpet for in here; or that sideboard, I remember they went and bought that together. But on the whole he didn't take a lot of interest in the home. He worked to provide the rent and furniture for it, but in his spare time he liked to go to the pub or football matches with his mates. I'm not saying he was unkind; he wasn't. Just somehow, well, distant I suppose'd be the word.

When I was little he was mostly still in the army, but I do remember once or twice when he came home on leave. One day I was playing in the street out there and I saw this soldier coming along; when he reached me, he suddenly picked me up and carried me up the stairs and along the balcony outside to our door. For quite a few minutes I didn't know who he was or what he was doing. It'd be the uniform, not having seen him for such a long while I suppose.

Oh yes and there's another occasion I remember him coming back on leave, I think it was for a week-end perhaps. He'd brought a couple of mates with him, two other soldiers; they came in unexpected while we were all sitting round the table in the kitchen eating our tea. Everybody was talking for a bit, then he suddenly leaned over and picked me up in his arms, and he said to his mates 'This one's my very favourite one.' I think that was awful.

I don't mean I thought it was awful then, no; I suppose I was pleased. But looking back on it now I do, that he should single out one of the four kids like that, in front of all the others. I mentioned it to Shirley once a few years back, but she says she doesn't remember it; so I don't suppose it can have done much harm. I still don't think he ought to have done it though.

My mother never would have: she'd never have admitted she liked one of us better than the others, ever. I used to try and get her to, often enough, when I was little; I can remember saying she must like one of us the most. But she wouldn't have it, she said she didn't; she said she always liked all four of us exactly the same; she always had and she always would.

And I really do think that was true, you know; I think she

honestly did feel like that. I remember saying to her once, it'd be about a couple of years before she died, I said something about Mary; that if I ever got married and had another one, I was sure I wouldn't be able to like him or her anything like so much. But Mum said, 'Oh you would, Ann, you know; however different he or she was, and in whatever way, you'd find it'd make no difference to you at all, you'd think just as much of any other child you had as you do of Mary.' So perhaps she was being honest that other time, you know; really and truly honest, that time when she said she didn't prefer one of us to the others.

I used to think she must sometimes, of course. If I was having a row with Jack when I was a kid, or Shirley, or Pam, and Mum took their side instead of mine, I'd think it was because she liked them better than me. But not for long, the feeling didn't last for long; she'd never let it. She could get very cross with you if you were naughty, but she wouldn't carry it on, you know how I mean? An hour or so later it'd be over and forgotten.

Anything else up to five, well no, I don't think I can remember anything else much. I must have been a bit of a scruffy kid like any other, I should think. Except on Sundays: Sundays we always had to have our best clothes on and our hair nicely brushed. Mum wouldn't let us take a ball out on the street to play with, nothing like that. She and Dad weren't church-going people, but they were respectable like everyone else in these blocks; going out in the street on Sundays was something that just wasn't done.

Only one other thing, a silly thing really; I don't know why I should remember it. I must have been about three or four, but I remember sitting on the floor there playing with toys or something, and I suddenly looked up and saw Mum sitting at that table there writing a letter, and she was crying. It would be to Dad, I suppose; the war was over but he was still away with the army in Belgium then, I think; I expect she was feeling fed up and lonely. Now I come to think of it, that must have been the only time in my whole life I ever saw Mum cry. I wasn't put out by it; just went on playing, probably wondered what was the matter but no more than that.

And yet I suppose that's why I do remember it, because it was so unusual. She was always such a quiet jolly friendly sort of person usually. A bit on the plump side: well, to be honest, rather more than a bit. There was lots there to cuddle, you know what I mean? And what with Dad being a bit remote in his ways, she was always the one you turned to if you hurt yourself and were crying, she'd cuddle you until you were better.

That's it, that's about all up to five, and then after that I started going to school, so we'll leave that part till next time, shall we? Anyway, Mary's not disturbed us; I thought she might, she can be a little monkey sometimes, getting out of bed. Sounds as though she's gone fast asleep tonight for a change. I told her to be good and stop in bed, but she doesn't always, she's got a real little mind of her own you know.

Funny in a way, isn't it? I mean she's just five herself now, I wonder how much she'll remember of her own life up to this point, if somebody ever asks her when she's grown up? Not a lot more than I've done, I suppose.

Sure you wouldn't like me to make you some more tea before you go? Let me get your coat then: there we are. Right, toodle-oo, mind how you go now, take care, and thanks for coming. See you Friday, same time? Good, I'll look forward to it, I'll be ready.

*

Always ready. She closed the door firmly after she had brought the tray in: poured the tea, lit a cigarette, curled into the armchair. A plain green dress with three-quarter length sleeves, a line of self-coloured buttons down the front, trim small white collar and cuffs. Levelly and straight, she smiled.

—Jack wanted to watch something on the telly tonight, I told him he could miss it for once. I think he's sitting in his room doing his stamp collection: he can keep an ear open for Mary, put her back in bed if she starts getting up to any of her tricks. We won't be disturbed. You don't look as tired tonight; I thought after you'd gone last time, you must get fed up of listening to people sometimes, I'm sure I would.

We finished before at when I started going to school, didn't we? I don't remember a lot about my first school, the one I went to until I was eleven. It's just up the road from here; I often walk past it now and honestly I do, I find it impossible to imagine I went there every day for five or six years when I was a kid. I don't remember the lessons, the teachers, nothing about it at all.

Sometimes I think I'll go in to it one day when I'm passing, just to have a look, and see if it does bring back any memories. You know, now I couldn't even tell you what it looks like inside, how the classrooms are arranged, which one I was in, or anything. All that time, all those years; the hours and hours I must have spent running about in that playground even. But when I walk past it, it just looks like a school to me, that's all; any other school you see when you're walking along a road. I've got no feeling of being connected with it myself when I was a kid there once.

It must be because I was a bit of a dunce I suppose, I mean that it made no impression on me. Perhaps that's a bit strong, I wasn't all that bad I suppose; but I wasn't exactly what you might call brilliant. Always somewhere round about the middle, nearer the bottom than the top half of the class. Spelling was the only subject I was much good at, and the days we went swimming to the baths were the only ones I could say I really enjoyed. I liked swimming very much, I used to have all sorts of fancy ideas those days about being a cross-channel swimmer when I grew up.

I must have been a very tomboyish sort of girl, now I come to think about it. Didn't play with dolls or anything of that sort, always preferred my brother's toys, his forts and soldiers and motor-cars. And roller-skates, that was something else I was very keen on. Never had a doll's pram, for instance, at least not that I can remember, or a doll.

Oh yes and my name, that was another thing; I couldn't stand that at all. You see it wasn't really Ann, it was Annette; and I was always scared to death the other kids might find out. Don't you worry about silly things when you're a kid? I don't know why I hated it so much; Annette seemed to me a very girly sort of name and I didn't think of myself as a girly girl, if you know what I mean. I liked the name Ann much better; it sounded plain and straight, Annette always seemed a bit fancy, I didn't feel it suited me at all.

What would I sooner have been called? Well, that's easy: Mary. That always has been my favourite name for a girl.

There's a song, isn't there? 'Her name was Mary, Mary: Mary is the name that I adore'. It goes something like that, I remember singing it to myself sometimes when I was little, wishing it was my name.

I can't think what made Mum call me Annette; it's not as though we've got the name anywhere in the family or anything. I suppose she just fancied it, like I've always fancied Mary. It could have been something else, though. Perhaps this sounds a bit unkind; but there were people who didn't know her, who sometimes thought Mum was, well a bit kind of standoffish and snobby. She wasn't at all really, not in any way; but I know she could give that impression. Ordinary working-class people are funny a bit sometimes about things: anyone trying to improve themselves, or make themselves in any way even just a little bit different with names or things like that.

For instance when she came up to school in the afternoons to collect me, sometimes she wore a hat. None of the other mums around here did, except perhaps on a Sunday; so I suppose they thought she was trying to look a bit grand. And another thing too was that she never ever used bad language; whereas a lot of them were always effing and blinding, they did it all the time without thinking. That was something Mum was very strict about; not only for herself but for all the rest of us as well, she wouldn't have bad language used in the house. And dropping your aitches, that was something else: she'd always tick you off about that and always be telling you to try and talk nicely.

But she definitely wasn't a snob, I mean she didn't feel she was better than anyone else. She just had certain standards about cleanliness and things, how you looked and how you spoke, and she brought us all up to try and keep to them. I think she was right too; she certainly taught me how to behave, to dress neatly and pronounce my words properly, even though I know I still have got a bit of a London accent.

Anyway, I was supposed to be talking about school, wasn't I? Can't remember much more about it, really. I know I ran away once or twice. Not from school, from Shirley and Pam when they were taking me in the morning. I'd sometimes run back here and stand outside the front door so they'd have to come back for me; or other times I'd hide round the back of one of the other blocks of flats, they'd have to come hunting for me all over the place. I didn't do it because I didn't like school, it was only meant to annoy them. And it did, too: I tell you, a right little devil I was really sometimes.

They'd get so annoyed about it if I did it too often to them, they'd complain to Mum about it, and she'd give me a smack for it. I deserved it; I'd do the same myself with Mary if she started doing things like that. It was rotten for Mum you know, four kids to look after on her own and Dad away in the army, I can't think how she put up with it the way she did. I never knew her lose her temper though: if you were naughty you got smacked, hard too sometimes, but it wasn't done in anger. It was for your own good, an hour later she'd give you a kiss and a cuddle to show you it was over and done with as far as she was concerned.

She never smacked you unless there was a good reason; you'd have to have been deliberately naughty. It wasn't to relieve her own feelings because she was annoyed about it herself. I remember one time she sent me out to do some shopping for her, I must have been eight or nine, she gave me a ten shilling note to go and get some groceries. Down at the bottom of the road there I met a boy, I suppose he'd have been thirteen or so, he saw me with this money in my hand and asked me where I was going. When I told him, he said he'd go and do the shopping for me; if I gave him the money he'd get the things and bring them back to the corner and he'd bring me some sweets as well. Course I never saw him again, did I? I was standing waiting for him for hours, it must have been nearly teatime, it was getting dark; and Mum had to send Pam or Shirley out to find me and fetch me back home. When I told her what had happened she gave me a right telling-off for being so stupid, but she didn't smack me for it. I realise now it was a lot of money to her; we weren't all that well off, she had to be very careful about every penny, it must have made a real dent in the housekeeping money. But that's an example of what I mean: where there'd have been good reason for her to get cross and smack me, but she didn't. Nothing else much I can think of about that first school.

I don't half keep wandering off the subject, don't I? A few friends I had there, a few special ones: five of us there was actually, we always used to play about together in a gang. Just silly kids' games round the streets, hide and seek, knocking dollies out of bed, that sort of thing. 'Knocking Dollies Out of Bed'? All kids play it, I suppose it's called different things in different parts of the country, is it? Pieces of cotton fastened from the front door knocker of one flat, across the passage to the front door of the flat opposite; you knock on one, then you all run off and hide down at the end, and watch. When the woman opens her door she can't see anyone, so she shuts it again. That makes the knocker bang on the door of the opposite flat: the woman in that one comes and opens her door, she can't see anyone, so she shuts it; and that bangs the first woman's door knocker again; sometimes they don't catch on for ages.

With big flat-blocks like these, we used to fasten the cotton up all over the shop; miles of it across the balconies from one side of the courtyard to the other, round corners, even down from one floor to another. It was really funny sometimes, we'd get half-a-dozen different door knockers banging away all together at once. Terrible, kids, aren't they, the things they get up to? It was, it was good fun though, even though I don't suppose I'd think it was myself if the kids started doing it to me now. Seems to have died out somehow though, you hardly ever hear of it, funny that isn't it?

We did, we had some good times together, all five of us. I remember all their names, every one of them in that little gang of ours. Patsy Scott, Maureen Marsh, Joan Golding, Vera Hurst and me. They all still live round about here too, except Joan Golding, she's up north somewhere I think. Patsy's married, and so's Maureen; I don't know whether Vera is or not, I haven't seen her for a bit. We're not close friends now; that was twenty years ago nearly, we've grown up and gone our different ways, even though we live in the same area still. You see one of them in the street when you're out shopping on a Saturday or something, but you don't really connect her with a little girl you were at school with yourself. It's better to keep it like that, I think; just a pleasant memory of a happy time a long while ago.

Well, I'm afraid that's all I can think of up till when I was eleven and went on to the elementary school, so would that be a good place to break off again? Next time I'll be telling you about what, from when I was eleven until I left school at fifteen, would you think? All right, yes.

You didn't have a coat tonight, did you, it's been nice and warm this week hasn't it? Toodle-oo then, mind how you go, take care, see you on Tuesday.

I don't suppose you could come Monday instead by any chance, could you? Well if you're sure it's not putting you out, yes to be quite honest I'd sooner you did come on Monday, yes. Now I've got used to talking to you, you see, I'd much sooner get it over as quickly as possible: the part of my life between eleven and fifteen, I mean.

It's not a time I'm very proud of, I'm afraid; I shall feel very embarrassed talking about it, the longer I have to wait before we get to it, the more I shall worry about it. So if you're quite sure Monday won't put you out, the earlier I do get round to telling you about it the better.

Right, good, thanks very much then; we'll make it Monday, right, thanks.

*

—I don't know where he's gone, I told Jack I didn't care where he went, just so long as he went out while we were talking tonight. I told him straight, I said I definitely didn't want him to be in the flat.

I've got Mary tucked up in bed early, she's fast asleep, I had a peep in at her just before you came. I've shut her bedroom door tight, I'll shut this one now, and then we'll be all right. I've made a good big pot of tea for us; help yourself if you want any more when you've finished that cup, because I shall probably forget to ask. Where did I put my cigarettes, have I got matches and everything, yes that's right. You comfortable all right there?

Well. Now then. This is it then, isn't it? We've come to it now. Yes. My life from eleven to fifteen. Well. Look, I'd better say this now before we start; I've never talked to anybody about this in all my life before. Perhaps I ought to have done, it'd probably been better if I had. But anyway there it is, I haven't.

Do you want any more tea? Do help yourself if you do, won't you? Yes right, now, well; I suppose I'd better just start at the beginning and tell you the whole lot, hadn't I? All right.

I think I'd find it easier if I didn't look at you while I talked, would you mind? I'll turn myself sideways in the chair like this and look at the fireplace. Yes, that's better. Right, from eleven then. From eleven.

While she talked she lit cigarettes one after another, without interval, one from the still glowing butt of the old. She never used nor needed the matches, and she did not drink her tea. She did not smile levelly or straight. She did not smile. She spoke to the fireplace in a monotone.

—When I was eleven I moved to the elementary school. It's the one round the back here, Ermine Road; I think it's a comprehensive now, but in those days it was just an ordinary secondary school. Fairly big, boys and girls mixed; about forty or more in each class.

You had all the ordinary subjects like arithmetic, geography, history, English and history and so on: then when you got higher up the school, the boys did woodwork and metalwork while the girls did cookery, shorthand, typing and a bit of book-keeping. I can't say I enjoyed any of them specially; and I hadn't got any particular ambitions. School was just a place you went to, to learn to read and write until you were old enough to leave at fifteen and start working for your living.

It'd be some time during that period my Dad came home out of the army and went to work on the 'buses. I think when the other children got past school-leaving age and started work, Mum herself got a bit of a part-time job too, cleaning; five mornings a week, something like that. More to occupy herself than anything else, though the bit of extra money was helpful as well of course. So that would be how it was when the trouble started with me, I should think.

By the time I was thirteen, all the other three had left school and were working. Jack would be what, about nineteen, he was in an engineering factory. Pam was seventeen, she worked in an office, I think it can only have been for about a year, then she got married. Shirley had left school and gone straight into a job as a waitress. So I was the only one left at school then, and I felt utterly fed up about it. There they all were, earning their own livings and with money in their pockets; they could more or less please themselves about what time they came in at

night, they could all go where they liked and do what they
wanted. They all seemed grown up and free; I was the only
one who was still a kid and who had to do what she was
told.

I did, I really hated it, being in that position. I started to be
very rebellious. I was always getting in trouble at school for
not paying attention in class or not doing my homework. At
home I used to have rows with Mum and Dad because I had to
be in by nine o'clock at night still. I'm not saying my parents
were over-strict, because they weren't. Now, I can see they
were absolutely right: but I didn't think so then. I couldn't see
it that way at all, I just felt very sorry for myself, and that life
was very rotten and unfair.

After a bit I started playing truant from school: not often,
only now and again. There was me and two other girls, Jessie
Stevens and Angela Rigby. They both lived in the block of flats
opposite to this one. One day we all decided we weren't going
to school the following Monday, just to see what happened.
We met outside the school gate in the morning, then instead of
going into the playground like all the others we peeled off and
spent the day wandering about the streets. We played about
round the railway yards, and on the swings in the park: anything we could think of, to pass the day till it was time to go
back home again as though we'd been at school like normal.

None of our parents twigged, so as far as we were concerned
that much was all right. All we had to worry about was what
would happen when we turned up at school the next day and
were asked where we'd been. But in fact when it came to it,
nobody at school asked us: they hadn't even noticed none of
the three of us was there the previous day. So we got right
away with it.

Naturally after that we thought if we could do it once we
could do it again. A few weeks later the whole school was
supposed to be going on a day-trip somewhere; I think it might
have been to look round the Tower of London or something
like that. Us three decided we didn't want to go; so we took
another day off, we disappeared and spent that one wandering
about on our own too. Again nobody found out about it, not
our parents nor the school.

It was only about once or twice a term we did it, perhaps for
a year. Then we started getting a bit more ambitious I suppose

you would call it, or adventurous. At least that's how we looked at it then: downright bloody stupid I'd call it myself now, looking back on it from this age. Anyhow, we got to thinking playing truant was all right; but it was a bit boring because we weren't doing anything except wander about all day. So eventually we decided we'd go to the seaside for a change, have a day in Margate, make it into a real proper adventure.

Of course for that we needed money, to pay for our fares on the train, buy ourselves sweets and things when we got there. Jessie and Angela were in the same position in their families as I was, they'd got elder brothers and sisters working too. We all agreed we'd try and get about a pound each for expenses. I pinched mine here at home; a few shillings out of Jack's money that he kept in a tin in his bedroom, some out of Shirley's handbag or Pam's, a bit out of my Mum's purse, and I think a few bob out of a pair of Dad's trousers he'd left lying around with loose change in one of the pockets. Taking it from here and there like that, nobody noticed it'd gone.

I suppose Jessie and Angela got their money the same way or similar. Anyway it all ended up the way we'd planned it; the three of us had about a quid each, and we took ourselves off to Margate for the day. When we got there we went on the pier, played with the slot-machines, stuffed ourselves with sweets, and then came home like normal. Three little innocents; and once again we got away with it.

These things always develop, don't they, once they start? The next time, the next thing we did, was even worse. I think if I remember right that had got something to do with a school trip as well. The whole school was going off for three days somewhere, out in the country; it might have been an exchange with another school or something of that sort. I'm not sure which one of us it was now, I think it might have been Jessie whose idea it was in the first place that we wouldn't go on the school trip; we were going to go off on our own for three whole days and nights instead. I think it was Jessie; she said she'd got an auntie or someone, who lived on a farm somewhere up in Essex, if we went there and said it was school half-term she'd put us up.

We all got our cases packed at home as though we were going on the school trip. This time we'd got the money off our parents to pay for it as though we were officially going with the school; then the three of us went off on our own like we'd planned. We went to Liverpool Street Station, caught a train to the nearest town to the place in Essex where Jessie said her auntie's farm was; then when we got there, we caught a 'bus out to one of the villages that Jessie thought it was somewhere near.

Of course it was all a shambles, the whole thing. Nobody'd ever heard of the farm, nobody'd heard of Jessie's auntie; we were in the wrong place altogether. The other two seemed to think it was a big laugh, but I didn't; I was fed up, I wished I'd never started out on such a stupid thing, I was really right miserable at it all, specially since it was coming on dark. We didn't know where we were, we'd nowhere to sleep, nothing; we ended up in a barn, sleeping on some hay.

I was woken up in the morning by a herd of cows mooing outside. I was scared to death I was, and cold and hungry. The other two were still fast asleep, and I decided there and then I'd had enough of it, I was going back home. I crept out of the barn with my things in my case, climbed through a hedge out on to the road, and after a bit a chap in a van pulled up and asked me where I was going and did I want a lift. I said I wanted to get back to London as soon as possible: he was very nice about it, he drove me all the way to the town where the station was, so I could catch a train.

I must have got back home round about lunchtime I should think. I knew the only thing I could do was face it out, own up to everything and take what was coming to me. But I didn't dare come straight in though: instead I came along the outside balcony to the front door, left my case outside and ran off again, down into the fields round at the back. Of course they knew where I'd be. After a bit Dad came down looking for me to take me back home. I remember he said as we were coming along the road Mum was so upset she didn't want to see me when we got inside; I was to go into my room and stay there until I was sent for.

I did, and I could hear him and Mum talking in here for ages, very quietly so I couldn't make out what they were saying, while they discussed what to do. Then Dad came and said she was ready for me to come in.

I can still see it now. She was in that chair, she didn't look at me or say anything, just sat absolutely silent. Then she got up very slowly, and picked up Dad's belt which he'd left lying on the table; and then she gave it to me. About six or seven right wallops across my backside; then she told me to go back in my room and stay there the rest of the day. A bit later she brought me something in to eat on a tray, just put it down and walked out without saying anything: then later on still when it was evening, she came and knocked at the door and told me it was time to get undressed and go to bed.

Like I've told you, being the person she was, the next day everything was back to normal again. She called me to get up for breakfast, perfectly ordinary and friendly and kind, and she never referred to the matter at all again.

And this now is what's so dreadful about it, you see. Because even after that I hadn't learned my lesson. That time of course the school had found out about it, and they made a big fuss; but Mum went down and talked to them. She said she'd dealt with me herself, and she thought I'd learned my lesson.

Only it was terrible: I hadn't.

I think in my last year at school I played truant a couple more times for a day along with the other two; then in my last term there was the worst thing of all. Was it Jessie, no I think it was Angela this time: she turned up at school one day and said she'd got her auntie's front door key; you know, the front door key to her flat. She said her auntie was out at work all day, if we went round there after school in the afternoon no one'd be at home, and she knew her auntie kept money hidden in her bedroom.

So that's what we did: after school was finished the three of us went to her auntie's flat, and Angela opened the front door with the key and we went in. Once we were inside the others were so scared they wanted to turn round and run away out again. And it was, it was me; I was the one who said now we'd got there we weren't going to leave without what we'd gone for. It was me who asked Angela which was the bedroom; it was me who went into it; it was me who searched through the drawers of the dressing-table till I found the money tucked away at the back behind her clean underclothes. And it was me who took it, the bundle of notes, and put it on the bed and counted them out equally between the three of us. There must have been about twelve or thirteen pounds altogether; I know it worked out we had about four pounds each.

I don't think we got a chance to spend it on anything much, we were all so scared we ran out as fast as we could and split up and went back to our homes. A few sweets, I think we went to the pictures the next night on it and bought some ice-cream and things, that was about all. I suppose it was a couple of days before Angela's auntie found out it was missing and started asking questions of the rest of her family. She soon found out what had happened and who was responsible; of course Angela owned up when they faced her with it, she told them who else had been involved, naturally.

Her mother came to see mine; Mum asked me about it, I handed over what I'd still got left of the money, and Mum and Dad made up what was short; Angela's auntie did get it all back in the end, every penny of it.

After Angela's mum had left there was another long conference between Mum and Dad about what to do. I think that time Mum gave me about twelve with the strap. Dad said I'd end up in prison if I went on the way I was going. And he was, you know, he was quite right; I'm certain that's what would have happened eventually if they hadn't been so firm with me. That's where I would have been by now, there's no question in my mind about it at all, if it hadn't been for them. I'd have been for crime and prison, for the rest of my life.

But I couldn't see it at the time, you know, I just couldn't. Mum had hurt me with the strap, that was all I knew, she'd really tanned me hard with it that time. I was lying on my bed in my room afterwards, crying; after about half an hour she came in, and she sat down on the edge of the bed beside me. She put her hand out, and put it on my arm. And I shook it off; I turned right round to the wall with my back towards her. So she just got up again and went out of the room. I know I was in the wrong; and it must have hurt her so much that I did that. I can't, honestly I can't ever forgive myself: I never could, and I never have.

Well, there you are. I've got it over, I've told you about it. I can't say it's something I look back on with any pride at all, that period of my life. It's not been easy for me to tell you about it; but then I knew it wouldn't be, I've been dreading it for weeks.

I'm feeling rotten, I've got a splitting headache now and I'm really tired: would you mind if we didn't talk any more tonight? Thanks.

*

—Hello, hello, come in, nice to see you. We could, you know, couldn't we, we could almost set the clock by you. I was telling Jack before he went out tonight, he was going to the pictures with one of his mates from work, he said he was going to be late. I told him he ought to get himself organised, I think people always ought to be reliable about times and appointments.

Well, sit you down, I've even got the teapot ready filled for us tonight, I poured the water on three minutes ago, I knew it'd be safe to make it, it should be just nicely brewed now. Ginger biscuits?

She sat comfortably, and lit a cigarette, and she smiled.

—I'm afraid I was a bit short when you left last time; I'm sorry, I didn't mean to be rude or anything. By the time I'd finished telling you about all that business, I did, I felt really drained. I think I'd told you beforehand, hadn't I, I'd never talked about it at all to anyone. I feel much better though now it's over; I feel fine tonight. Go straight on from fifteen shall I, then; righty-oh.

I left school, and of course as soon as I did I was all right, I was grown up then, wasn't I? Now what was my first job; I wonder if I can remember them in the right order? It's going to be a bit difficult, because I know I had thirteen different jobs between the ages of fifteen and twenty-one, which is a lot really isn't it, it works out at more than two a year. Anyhow, all I can do is try, isn't it?

The first one was a shoe shop, now that I do remember, only I'm not sure which one. No wait a minute, I tell a lie; it wasn't a shoe shop either, it was a dress shop, yes that's it. Down the High Street: I'd only left school a few weeks, I saw a notice in their window saying they wanted a junior assistant so I went in and asked, and I got it. The money wasn't very good, only about just over three pounds a week, but anyway it was a start. I stayed there not long, I shouldn't think it was more than

about five or six weeks; then that was when I went into the
shoe shop, yes, because the money was another five bob or so
more.

The shoe shop, I was there I should say about six months,
perhaps a bit longer: then I went into an office, junior filing-
clerk, I think that was a job I saw advertised in the paper. That
was a bit boring, but I stuck it out more or less a year or so
until I couldn't bear it no longer. I think I must have got
something of my Dad in me, you know; I wasn't happy doing
regular hours in the same place with the same faces all the
time, I wanted to be out and about and mixing with people.

So eventually, yes that's right, it was while I was still working as a filing-clerk I went and applied to go on the 'buses as a
conductress. I was, I was so disappointed when they told me
they wouldn't have me because I was still too young. I didn't
know what to do, I was really fed up. Anyway luckily for me
there was another girl in the office, she felt exactly the same
way as I did. She said as soon as she could the next spring, she
was going to start writing round hotels and see if she could get
herself a job for the summer as a chambermaid or waitress. I
had a talk with Mum and Dad about it, and they agreed; so I
asked her while she was at it to try and get two jobs in the
same hotel, one for herself and one for me.

Well, it wasn't long before we were lucky; she didn't have to
write to too many places before she found somewhere that did
have two vacancies for the summer. It was in Torquay, one of
the big hotels there, it was very nice indeed. A lovely summer
we had that year too, the weather was marvellous; we went
about April or May, and stayed on right through to the end of
September.

I enjoyed it all except the being away from home part; that
was the only bit of it I didn't like. I used to write letters every
week, sometimes twice a week; Mum and Dad came down and
stayed in a boarding-house for a week once, and another time
they came for a week-end as well. But I did get a bit lonely
now and again, I must admit; in fact there were times I
thought I wouldn't be able to stick it out because I was so
homesick. Anyway, I managed it somehow; and I think the
experience was good for me, it helped me be a bit more
independent and stand on my own feet.

I met some nice people down there too; you know, others

like me who were doing holiday jobs. There was an Irish girl
called Sheila who was a waitress, a boy called Ron who was a
kitchen porter, his girl friend Peggy who worked at one of the
other hotels, and a few others. There was quite a group of us
altogether, we used to have some really good fun; we did a lot
of swimming on our afternoons off, went to dances sometimes
if four or five of us could get the same evening free together.
On the whole it was very nice, and it did definitely make me
grow up a bit, because up till that time I'd never ever been
away from home at all really.

All good things have got to come to an end some time
though, don't they? By the end of the holiday season I was
back here again, living at home and looking for another job.
Now then, what came next; I think it was another shoe shop.
Yes it was: only in that one I had more responsibility, I did
some of the clerical work and they put me up to cashier after a
while. I'd be seventeen or so by then. And what came after
that, why did I leave there?

Oh yes of course, that was when Dad died; yes, that was
why I had to leave that job, because the money was so poor.
With Dad dying, Mum was having a hard time keeping up the
flat, making both ends meet over the rent and food and things.
I think she got some insurance money and a bit from the 'bus
people, but it wasn't going to be enough; we decided I really
would have to try hard and get something that was better
paid.

That was the time I began to wish I'd paid a bit more
attention to my lessons when I was at school, gone to night
school afterwards to improve my shorthand and typing, and
perhaps get one or two certificates for it. That would certainly
have made things a lot easier for me in trying to get a better
job if I'd done something like that.

Anyway finally I had to settle for office work again, with a
big wholesale grocers in the City. Usual thing, filing and
clerical work, very very boring: but the money was good, quite
good I mean for somebody like me, with no qualifications at
anything, and that was the main thing, the money. That lasted
I should say about six months, then I had a whole string of
jobs one after the other, none of them lasting more than a few
months each. The reason for the changes was that every new
one paid a bit more, so at least I felt I was making a bit of

progress financially, even though they were all so dead boring.

I was on the reception desk at a firm of clothing manufacturers, then a clerk with a biscuit company, a cashier in a
newspaper wholesalers, an order clerk for an electrical equipment firm, a sort of invoice-typist-telephonist and general
dogsbody at another newspaper wholesale place; then finally a
showroom assistant in a furniture shop. The money there still
wasn't all that brilliant, but you did get a commission on sales
which helped it up into quite a decent sum most weeks.

Have I got them all now, just let me count them out on my
fingers ... yes that's right, that's all twelve. And then by the
time I was twenty-one I'd got the thirteenth, which was the
lucky one for me. It was the one I'd always wanted; which was
one on the 'buses.

I liked that, it did, it suited me right down to the ground. It
could get a bit hectic sometimes, especially in the rush hour if
you were on a route that went through the middle of London;
and once in a while you'd get a passenger being a bit stroppy,
but apart from that it was ideal. You had to work quite a bit of
extra shift work to get your overtime up to make it into a
decent week's wage, but I was young and fit and strong and in
good health. Being on your feet all day could get a bit tiring
sometimes, but you never minded because of all the compensa-
tions like not working the same hours day after day, and
always being busy and among all kinds of different people,
always knowing no two days were ever going to be the same in
succession.

I suppose a lot of people would think it more tiring than it
actually is; but I never found it like that. I mean, I was able to
keep working right up until about nine or ten weeks before I
had Mary; and I think I'd have gone on a bit longer than that
even, if it hadn't been for Mum saying she thought it'd
probably be wiser if I stopped, because of the risk of slipping on
the stairs or straining myself trying to push my way through if
I'd got a heavy load of passengers on. That was typical of her
of course, keeping an eye on my health all the time.

I had Mary in the hospital and the confinement wasn't too
bad, I was back home again in about ten days. Mum came in
the late afternoon and fetched us from the hospital in a taxi.
When we got to the front door out there she opened it with her
key, then she told me to go in ahead of her and turn the light

on in the hall. It was so dark I could hardly see a thing; and when I did find the light and switch it on, do you know what they'd done? There was a big notice pinned up across the passage, right from one side to the other, about that high. It said 'Welcome Home, Ann and Mary.' And all the others, Jack and Shirley and Pam and their husbands, and all our friends and neighbours, they'd all been hiding behind the doors and then they came rushing out from all over the place to greet us. And we had a really marvellous party, lots of food and everything; it was, it was really smashing, a lovely home-coming.

I went back to work on the 'buses after, it'd be when Mary was about four or five months old I suppose. Mum looked after her for me when I wasn't here, she was marvellous about nights and things. You know, if I was on early turns or some-thing, she'd have Mary's cot in her room so she could see to her in the night if she cried, and I wouldn't be disturbed. It's one of my biggest regrets, you know; I don't suppose by the time she's grown up Mary'll even remember anything about Mum at all. Since she died, the lady in the flat underneath this one on the floor below has had Mary for me during the day; she's very good, she's got two children of her own and she and her husband are both very nice people. But it's not the same, quite, is it really, as Mary having her own grandma, I mean?

Other regrets? No, not really: well, only two, I suppose. On the whole I think I've been very lucky, certainly as far as having Mary's concerned; she's a lovely kid, she is really, there's nothing in the world I wouldn't do for her. Mind you, I shan't spoil her you know; I mean I learned the right way to bring up children from Mum. You've got to be firm and very strict sometimes, because it's for the child's own good in the long run even though they don't see it that way themselves at the time.

I was saying wasn't I about regrets, about having only two. One's such a little one it's hardly worth mentioning. It's just that, well, I suppose I've got to face it: the trouble I started last year with my back, the doctor said it was simply making it worse all the time doing a standing up moving about job like 'bus conductress, it was essential I got myself work sitting down in an office. So that's what I'm doing now.

It's quite a responsible job, the pay's good enough for us to live on; in fact with bonuses and things I suppose you could say it was quite generous. But I think if I'm going to be absolutely honest with myself, I must say I'm kidding myself a bit; pretending one day my back'll be all right again, and I'll be able to go back to being a conductress. Because I'm speaking the plain truth now when I say that honestly I don't think it ever will.

Still, as I said, that's only a little regret, I think I can live with it. After all, I shall have to, shan't I? The other one though, the big one: I'll have to admit I do find that one much more difficult to live with.

Well, it's what I told you about before, once, a bit: about the nights I used to go to the hospital and sit by Mum's bed when she was unconscious. It's that I couldn't speak to her then, and tell her how sorry I was for having hurt her that time she'd strapped me and when she sat on my bed I'd turned away; how ashamed of myself I was that after all she'd done for me I'd actually gone and stolen money, I'd actually been a thief. And I wanted to tell her so much, even though I had turned my back on her that time, that it hadn't meant at all that at that moment I didn't really love her.

Even though she was unconscious, I did try; I did try to say it, though I knew she wouldn't be able to hear it. I did try to speak and put it into words. But you know, I just couldn't. I'm afraid I'm not the sort of person who talks very easily about things like love.

*

CHAPTER FOUR

PENNY STANNERS

What's a girl supposed to do if she feels sexy, or is that only allowed for men?

—I was doing some shopping one afternoon last week on my way back here from my mother's, and I had Timmy in the pram. In the street I bumped into a woman I haven't seen since I was in the sixth form with her daughter at the County High, five or six years ago. 'Why, it's Penny!' she said, 'I'd recognise you anywhere! How simply marvellous to see you again, how *are* you?' Fine I said, fine, I was at teacher-training college now. Well, good Lord, she said, I still looked as though I was eighteen. Then she looked at Timmy sitting up in his pram. 'Oh, isn't he beautiful!' she said. 'But gracious, don't tell me he's yours, is he?' He most certainly was, I said; why, didn't she think he looked like me? 'Oh, yes, of course he does!' she said. 'Absolutely the spitting image! How wonderful though, oh, aren't you lucky to have such a gorgeous baby! But doesn't time fly, I mean it seems only last week you and Helen were in Miss Martin's class at school together. I've often thought about you, Penny, because you were one of Helen's very best friends, she'll be so thrilled when I tell her I've seen you. But honestly, I just can't get over it; you know, I mean, well we didn't even know you were married!'

'I'm not,' I said.

'Oh,' she said, 'Oh really ... well, erm ... oh.' Anyway, she said, it had been absolutely wonderful to run into me again, right out of the blue like that, really marvellous; now I was around she was sure she'd see me again, and when she did we'd fix up a proper meeting so we could have a really good chat: only unfortunately just then she was in a frantic rush, she was nearly half an hour late for an appointment which she *had* to keep ... she scooted off as though she was frightened she might catch some kind of infectious illness if she stopped near me any longer.

*

A gently sarcastic snort, a faint smile. She stabbed out her cigarette rhythmically as though it was a dagger, in the ashtray on the arm of her chair; when she bent forward to pick up her mug of coffee from the floor in front of her the unpinned raven-dark curtain of her hair closed across her face. Sitting up, a quick movement with the back of the fingers of one hand swept it away again behind her shoulders, clear of her small porcelain-doll cheeks and her round doe-brown velvet eyes.

Penelope Stanners, student teacher, age 23. Only just over five feet high, and talking with frequent mischievous laughs and glances, and gesticulating hands. A slender body in a bright orange and brown floral-print dress of minuscule length with matching pants beneath. Rarely still, sliding out of the confines of the chair and perching cross-legged on the end of her bed, or moving again before long to lie full length on her stomach on the floor with a cushion under her elbows, propping up her chin on her clasped hands. Green eye-shadow, long curling eyelashes, pretty, animate, carefree.

*

Other times, she wore a dirty old fawn jumper, and a shapeless grey tweed skirt and heavy-rimmed glasses; her hair was pinned back against her head and fastened tightly in an untidy bunch of wisps and straggling ends. No make-up on her face, her lips pale and thin and her cheeks white; heavy-lidded, silent for long periods, she pulled hard at her cigarettes, not noticing when what remained of them burned at her fingers as she stared into past and future as though both were sterile empty bowls. Once, then, she had defined the duality.

—Oh definitely two persons. And I don't know which is the real me; or whether it's both for that matter, or neither. Perhaps there's a third one, a kind of synthesis, something quite different trying to emerge. Sometimes I hope there is, sometimes I hope there isn't; and sometimes when I'm feeling really bad, I really don't care. Like I am tonight, I don't care at all much, one way or the other.

Do you know Sylvia Plath's poems? There's one called 'Lady Lazarus', I think it is: that says more exactly than anything else I've read how I feel. I've got it somewhere, let me see if I can find it, I'll read it you. Yes, it's here.

> 'Dying
> Is an art, like everything else.
> I do it exceptionally well.
> I do it so it feels like hell.
> I do it so it feels real.
> I guess you could say I've a call.'

She lived with her three year old son in a small furnished self-contained flatlet on the first floor of an old house.

*

—I know I look good tonight; I feel good. I'm on the way up again for a while, thank God. When you're not, it's like being in a river; you're swept along by the current, helpless, you can't do anything. Then if you're lucky, you catch hold of the branch of an overhanging tree or something, pull yourself up out of the water somehow and flop onto the bank. You lie there a bit, then you realise you're on dry land. A funny feeling, I can't explain it; but somehow you know you're going to be all right from then on.

Had anything to eat, would you like me to make you an omelette; go on, say yes, good, I like making them. Fuck it, where the bloody hell's the frying pan? Come across a writer on sociology called Bernstein, ever? I'm just reading one of his books from the college library; he says working-class people have only a sort of 'general public' language to express themselves in, and it puts a tremendous restriction on their ability to think, because it limits the tools with which they intellectualise. So he says working-class children therefore on the whole tend to act things out, rather than think them out; whereas people in the middle class are better equipped to deal with problems by thinking them out, which is socially much more acceptable because it's less likely to be destructive.

I thought when I was reading it, 'Yes mate you're right; and who should know it better than me.' Perhaps that's got something to do with the two person thing I'm always telling you about. I wonder if it has? I not only feel like two people all the time, I bloody well *am* two people, there's no getting away from it, is there?

I'm the working-class girl who got out of it, got out of her background; and now I'm nearly in the professional-status middle class, which I don't really belong in at all. I hear them talking, some of the other students at college, and I think they've simply got no idea of what life's really like at all: all they've ever known is the suburban semi in Hendon where they were born and grew up. I couldn't ever stand living in that sort of an area; but whenever I do go back to the East End to see my mother, I don't feel I belong there any more either.

That incident I told you about the other week with the mother of the girl I was at school with: middle-class people do, they make me spit. But with working-class people too ... to them I'm not one of them any more. So where do I go from here? And as if that wasn't bad enough on its own, there's the whole woman/female thing on top, that makes me so different from most other girls, apparently.

Well hell, I always was mixed up; all right, I'm a problem. Or I was, perhaps I'm getting a bit better, now I'm a bit older and more capable of looking after myself. I was a problem for a long time, very well experienced at it, a fully paid-up member of the category. Unmarried mothers are a special separate column in the statistics.

I could always see it on social workers' faces nearly all the time: 'Here Is A Problem'. It wouldn't have been so bad for them if it'd be allowed to rest at that, but I wouldn't let it. Not married and had a baby: cleared up and solved. Thank you; thank you very much. But within a year, I was back on their doorsteps. ...

Here I am once more, I've done it again, I'm pregnant a second time. They didn't even bother to try to hide their expressions then: 'Now Here We Have A MAJOR PROBLEM'. And if it happens a third time, good God, what on earth are they going to say *then*?

Flippant, I suppose it sounds, doesn't it? It's just nerves really; the closer I get to tears the more I tend to laugh. I don't really think it's funny, not one little bit I don't; it's not funny at all. Oh well, when you've finished eating I'll make some coffee, then we'll settle down and go on.

*

My father was a stallholder in an East End market; he sold fruit and vegetables. He worked hard, and saved his money until he could buy a second stall; then he worked harder still and saved even more, and finally went into business properly, had his own shop, with living accommodation above. It was while he and Mum were there that they had my elder sister, Margaret. She was their only one: I don't properly know why, whether they planned it or it just happened. I do know for over ten years there was no question of them ever having another.

The three of them lived over the shop, and business was good. In ten years they'd got enough money to make a major step forward in life, and actually buy a house on a mortgage. That really was something if you were working-class. It was only over the other side of the river, not in a posh area or anywhere like that. But it was their own house, and I think they thought they were going to live in it happily ever after with their only child. Mum told me once, a few years ago it'd be now, I must have been conceived either the last night they spent in the flat over the shop, or the next night, which was the first one they spent in their new house.

I recall nothing special about my childhood. I was an ordinary happy kid, who everyone called 'Tich' for obvious reasons; and I loved both my Mum and Dad very much, and they were always very nice. Mum was affectionate and cheerful, a model of what mums should be; she kept me clean and tidy when she could, and didn't get too cross when she couldn't, which was quite often.

My sister Margaret was all right; we weren't terribly close to each other though, because there was such a difference in our ages. She left home to get married when I was ten. I was a bridesmaid, I had a lemon organza dress which I remember, with a blue sash and a little cap, and I carried a posy. I don't remember clearly but I think really I was quite pleased when she left home, because it meant I could have our bedroom entirely for my own. That made me feel very grown-up. I can't ever remember a sense of missing her or feeling lonely. She went to live in the Home Counties, where her husband was a factory worker and they'd been given a council flat near his job.

My Dad, well, he and I always got on very well indeed. He was enormously proud of me because I always did so well at school; he used to spend hours and hours in the evenings helping me with my homework. Though I say it myself, I was very bright: exceptionally bright I mean for the school and the area we lived in. There was never any question whatsoever about me not getting through the eleven-plus selection exam. When I took it I sailed through it: I did so well I was offered a place at a posh High School in one of the 'better' areas, right outside our normal world.

It meant a lot of travelling there and back every day; I suppose the fares alone must have been pretty expensive. But Dad didn't mind a bit; if there was ever anything I wanted or needed for school, like books or uniform or sports gear, he saw to it I got it. I suspect nothing in his whole life gave him greater pride than knowing he'd got such a clever daughter. It meant all the more to him because Margaret had never got anywhere at all at school, she was hopeless academically. With me, and as far as he and I suppose most other people too could see, there was no limit to where I might go. Certainly on to a university, I don't think there could've been much doubt about that. I was one of those fortunate types to whom learning and passing exams was no effort at all, I felt I'd been made for it.

But despite that, I wasn't at all happy at school, though. I think that was when my two-person business began. You see, I think it was a mistake I went to that school, so far out of my own area, and so far out of my own class. I was good at school work, that never bothered me, I could do it standing on my head; but I didn't get on with any of the other girls. Also I was on very bad terms with all the teachers, because I wouldn't ever do homework. When I got home in the afternoon, all I wanted was to get my school uniform off, and go roving round the streets with my mates, other girls and boys of my own age.

And I think the fact I used a lot of bad language and spoke with a common accent upset the teachers too; they were always correcting me and punishing me for it. They thought I was coarse and uncouth, which I was: and I thought they were stuffy and stuck-up, which they were. A total failure of communication, a complete lack of understanding of background and values and behaviour, between two entirely different social classes. My own feeling now is they were more at fault than I: they were adults, they should have been more tolerant and tried harder to understand. I was only an adolescent, preoccupied with the problems of growing up; any grasp of wider social concepts was beyond my capabilities at that stage.

What the outcome might have been, I don't know: presumably when I got to a university I'd probably have found life easier, because there'd have been others there, certainly at the redbricks, from similar backgrounds to mine. Unfortunately it never happened, because at the beginning of my final year at school, the one in which I was due to take my 'A' levels and then go to university, my father died.

His partner in the business bought up Dad's share; that money just about paid off what was owing on the house, leaving Mum without any other capital or income. She'd no qualifications or special abilities, she was well past fifty years old, and the best job she could get herself only brought in eight pounds a week. She was all for trying to struggle along so I could continue my education; but by that time I was so heartily sick and fed up with life at school, I jumped at having an excuse to leave and find myself a job.

Besides, I'd already had a taste of freedom, and I rather liked it. The idea of being an independent and self-supporting working girl, like all the rest of my friends in the area where we lived, rather appealed to me. By freedom I mean of course sexual freedom. In the summer holidays of that year we'd been for a fortnight to a holiday camp on the south coast. I met a boy who was staying there with two others, the three of them sharing a chalet. He and I took a great shine to each other, and all we wanted to do was be alone and make love. So his mates used to go off and leave us in the chalet in the afternoons, and we spent most of the time in bed in it.

I not only liked it very much, I couldn't have enough; the first couple of times while I was in the process of losing my virginity was a bit clumsy and awkward; but once that was accomplished I got to enjoy it more and more and more, I seemed to take to sex just as I took to education at school; no trouble at all, it was as though I'd been made for that too.

*

—When my father died I was seventeen. I got a temporary job as a clerk in an office in the City, then went to night-school on a crash course to learn shorthand and typing, so I could get myself better paid secretarial work as quickly as possible.

I missed him very much of course, and so did Mum: he was a very nice man, and a very kind man; for a long while the house seemed very empty and forlorn. It was much worse for Mum of course than it was for me: at least I had quite a decent job, and I always made lots of friends. One in particular was a boy called Nick, he worked in another office near the one I was in, and I went out a lot with him. He had a car, nothing very grand; but enough to take us wherever we wanted to go, which was usually to some out of the way place where we could get in the back seat together and make love.

I forget why we broke up; anyway we quarrelled about something, and we had a big dramatic scene which I ended very grandly by telling him I never wanted to see him again. Actually, though I'd never have let on to him about it, I think I was pretty keen on him; I know I went home afterwards and cried like hell.

About three weeks later, I've always been as regular as clockwork and I hadn't come on: I thought Oh Christ, that's just great that is, now I'm really in a spot. So I swallowed my pride and 'phoned Nick; I told him I was sorry for what I'd said, could we meet one evening after work for a drink, and try and make things up again? Of course he was suspicious immediately; he asked what was the matter, and why I should suddenly want to see him. I insisted it was simply that I wanted to make things up, and no more. He said no, he was sorry, but he was going out with another girl now.

I said it didn't matter; I'd be quite happy in that case if we could just go on being friends, but at least we could meet and have a talk. That must have more or less confirmed it, as far as he was concerned. He agreed to meet, but before I'd even a chance to open my mouth he said 'Don't tell me you've gone and got yourself pregnant, is that it?'

I couldn't blame him for being annoyed; I suppose he thought I was going to try and get him to marry me, or at least get some money out of him. I told him that I wasn't, I accepted things were finished between us; all I was asking was could he get some tablets or something of some kind that would bring me on. He said he'd try; I knew he had a friend who worked in a chemist's, I asked him to ask him for something. Weeks went by; Nick kept saying he hadn't been able to get in touch with his friend; then he met me one lunch-time and gave me a couple of pills which he said were supposed to be guaranteed to do the trick.

For all the difference they made, I should imagine they were aspirin. By now I was over two months overdue and getting pretty desperate. I thought the only thing to do was to tell Mum. When I did, I think she was a bit shocked at the idea I'd been having intercourse; but she married Dad when she was seventeen herself, so the idea wasn't too outrageous for her. She was absolutely splendid. She told me all the folk-myths and old wives' tales she could remember, and we tried every single one: drinking tumblerfuls of neat gin, jumping three times off a chair onto a hard floor, syringing with hot water, and half a dozen other things. But not one of them worked.

In the end I went to a doctor: he told me I was much too far gone for termination, and he passed me on to a local church welfare organisation. They sent a woman round to see me, and I should imagine she exemplified absolutely everything that a social worker shouldn't be. She was a spinster in her fifties, tut-tutting and dear-dearing all over the place; every time I mentioned any prospective difficulty of any kind, her standard response was 'Well you should have thought of that beforehand, shouldn't you?' Even if she'd not been like that, though, I don't think it'd have made much difference.

By that time, as far as I was concerned all I cared about was having it, since I'd apparently got to, then getting back to normal as quickly as possible. I thought of it entirely as though it was an illness, which was going to last for a while, and then I'd recover. All I asked the welfare worker to do was arrange practicalities: fix me up in a mother-and-baby home for six weeks before I was due and six weeks afterwards, and arrange for the baby to be adopted. I had a total of about fifteen minutes' chat with her, in which I made plain what I felt; then I left everything to her. That was the sum total of any social work I wanted.

I stopped on at work until I was over six months; then it was beginning to show, and make me feel physically uncomfortable. So after that I stayed at home, and Mum and I lived on what she could earn plus what the National Assistance allowed me. The first time I felt it move inside me was the first time too I think, that it ever struck me it was more than just an illness, and I was actually going to give birth to another human life.

At that stage then I had to do all sorts of mental somersaults. But it was still all up here in my head; I approached it as an intellectual problem, one that could be neatly sewn up and settled. I refused to let myself feel anything, or even think about it in any other way than as an unavoidable temporary inconvenience. When the time came for me to go there, I packed a small case and took myself off to the mother-and-baby home.

I think my mother did offer to look after me at home, but I was adamant I wanted to do it my way. I'd thought the home might be a bit grim; but in fact it wasn't, it was quite a good one. I enjoyed being there, as much as possible under the circumstances. Then from there I went into hospital to have the baby. I had a pretty awful labour because I'm small and it was big; I had a third-degree tear which wasn't very pleasant. It was a girl.

I hadn't made, and I wouldn't make, any preparations of any kind for the birth. Mum said I'd need a few clothes at least for the baby, while it was with me in hospital and at the home afterwards; but I wouldn't buy them myself. I asked her to go out and get whatever she thought would be the minimum necessary. While I was in the home, before I went into hospital, my sister came to see me one day and said she thought I'd probably find it less embarrassing in hospital if I was wearing a wedding-ring. So I simply asked her to buy me one at Woolworth's and bring it in on her next visit, which she did. It cost four and sixpence. I didn't think about names for the baby, or anything: I was determined to have nothing at all to do with it.

After it was born I wouldn't breast-feed it because I felt I might be in danger of getting emotionally involved if I did. As I said, I'd had this bad tear, so in fact I was in the hospital much longer than expected. I remember one day, I think it was the first day I was allowed out of bed to go and have a bath; I was sitting in the water and I suddenly saw it all starting to go bright crimson all round me. Very unpleasant; I was scared to death and went into a state of nearly total hysterical collapse.

But it had its benefits too, the long stay in hospital I mean. Because by the time I was ready to come out, all the adoption formalities had been fixed. It was possible by then for me to hand the baby over, literally at a meeting on the day I was discharged from hospital, to the couple who were having her. Having done that, there seemed no point in going back to the mother-and-baby home again, so I went back to my own home instead.

Mum looked after me for a few weeks until I'd recovered my strength. Then I started looking through the papers for a job. It wasn't long before I got one, and I went back to work again as a secretary for a firm of solicitors in the City. Working, earning a decent wage, new boy-friends; enjoying life to the full again, I was, and went on doing so for the next six or seven months.

Then one day I stopped at home because I was feeling rotten. Mum went off to work, and after she'd gone I settled down comfortably in the kitchen, with my head on a cushion inside the gas-oven, and turned the taps on. I think it must have been one of the neighbours who smelled the gas and broke a window and climbed in, and got an ambulance and all the rest of it.

*

—Tonight I'm a bit low: I've been this way for nearly a week now. I ought to have tidied up the room, and made a bit of an effort to tidy myself up too. But I didn't feel like it; what the hell anyway, why should I pretend?

That first time I tried to kill myself, I think it was the suddenness of it, most of all, that took me by surprise. It wasn't as though I'd been dwelling on the idea for days, or even hours, beforehand. It just suddenly swept over me, an irresistible desire to put an end to everything. Irresistible desires are things

I seem to be very susceptible to, one way or another.

At hospital they treated me, kept me in a few days, then referred me to their psychiatrist. He said I'd had a bad attack of post-puerperal depression and it was very common: he gave me some pills which he said would cure it: and they did. I was discharged within a week, and put under the care of a local G.P. who continued the treatment and prescribed me various other things as well, like tranquillisers and sleeping-pills.

I had a series of jobs, and a series of boy-friends. Eleven months after the first birth, I was pregnant again. So what with that and the suicide attempt, and the fact I'd already had one illegitimate child, I was the target for an army of social workers then. You're not supposed to do it twice, you're really not; once is permissible, twice is thoroughly irresponsible. And they don't like it a bit when you tell them yes, thank you, you know all about birth-control, but you can't be bothered to use it.

This time the bloke concerned was already married. I'd been to bed with him at a party; I think I'd only ever met him once before. It wasn't a relationship that meant anything to either of us, so I didn't even see any point in letting him know. If I had, he'd probably quite rightly have said it wasn't necessarily him, it could have been anyone out of about three or four others.

When I told Mum it'd happened again, she just broke down and cried. I can't say I blame her. I tried to make reassuring noises about how this time I'd definitely be getting an abortion, one of the social workers involved would fix it. But I must have known, even then, that it wasn't true: I'd no intention at all of doing it. I'd no intention of giving my baby away for adoption this time. I'd made up my mind that not only was I going to go ahead and have it, but I was going to keep it too.

I wasn't consciously aware that it was a replacement for the one I'd lost: it's only later when you come to look back on things that you see them that clearly. But I'd changed completely: the first time it'd all been thinking and rationalising. Now, the second time, it was purely feeling that was guiding me, not thought at all. I didn't know how it was going to work out, or even if it would; but I'd got an absolute determination that somehow I was going to make it do so.

My mother's health wasn't good; I didn't feel I could throw any more burdens on her. She'd been spending more and more time up at my sister's and was often out of London. So I thought the best thing I could do would be to leave home and try and get myself some kind of living-in job, with a family who'd have me with my baby after it was born.

I went to see the National Council for the Unmarried Mother and her Child, and they were really terrific in the help they gave me, both supportive and practical. They've always been very ready to help me ever since. I've known people who think the name is a bit off-putting, but I can't say it's ever worried me. I don't see it matters what it's called, so long as it does its job and fills a need, which it most certainly does. It was with their help that I did eventually manage to get myself settled with a middle-aged couple in South London who had two small children which I looked after during my pregnancy. I went back to them after I'd been in hospital to have Timmy.

This time I had a very quick and easy delivery; and this time I'd done all the right things, made preparations, bought a few clothes, even decided on a name for either a boy or a girl. I felt quite different too: this was my baby, it wasn't an abstract thing, he was a person who belonged to me and to whom I belonged as a mother.

But I suppose everything has its advantages and disadvantages; you never get one without the other. After a few months back with the couple in South London, I started getting very depressed again. I was often in floods of tears, and the rows between us about the amount of free time I was entitled to got increasingly frequent. I don't suppose either side was completely right or wrong; but I got more and more angry and resentful at being the recipient of kindness and charity, and increasingly determined to leave and find a place entirely of my own.

When I did, I lived for about six months in a series of different horrible furnished rooms, on National Assistance. It wasn't exactly luxury living, but it was enough to get by. What was increasingly worrying me, though, was that I felt I was absolutely wasting my life and getting steadily nowhere. I convinced myself that I'd made another terrible mistake: this time in deciding to keep Timmy. It would have been much better if I'd had him adopted too, there'd be far greater prospects for some kind of a decent future for him.

I'd amassed a fairly large collection of pills of all kinds from different doctors, particularly barbiturates. One night I sat down to assess, very coolly and calmly, the advantages and disadvantages to myself and Timmy of me dying or staying alive. As far as I could see my life was of minimal importance; and Timmy, I came to the conclusion, would be much better off without me in the long run.

You're very dispassionate when you're in that state of mind; once you've mentally solved a problem, you can get quite methodical about trying to carry it out. I packed all Timmy's things in a case, and I took it and him round to a church orphanage near where I was then living. It was very late at night: I went in and gave them a fictitious name and address, and said I'd got to catch the midnight train up to Birmingham to go and see my mother who was seriously ill; but I'd be back for certain the following day. Then I shot straight out again.

I went back to my room, got a glass of water, sat down on the bed, and swallowed the pills; about sixty altogether, very calmly, one after another. Then I lay down, feeling relaxed and at peace. I remember the drowsiness beginning to wash over me, it was like great big warm waves. I felt very happy at the thought that in a few hours I should be dead.

I think it's Erwin Stengel who says in a book of his I read about it, that a large proportion of suicides should be more correctly described as 'accidental deaths'. A lot of people who succeed in killing themselves don't really mean to; they leave a large element of chance in it, half hoping they won't succeed because someone will find them and save them. I think if that's true, which it probably is, then there ought to be another category called 'accidental lives' too, for cases like mine. I don't see how I could possibly have foretold that a boy I'd met casually at a party, four nights before, should have taken it into his head to call and see me at seven o'clock the next morning, as he was walking down the road on his way to work. The house front door was open; I'd closed the door of my room but not locked it, so after he'd knocked and got no reply he pushed it open.

The usual business: ambulance, hospital, stomach-wash, referral to psychiatrists and social workers, everybody trying to put the pieces together again. I must say Mum was tremendous: she insisted I went and lived back at home with her. A different hospital and different methods too: this time I had

psychotherapy twice a week, I went and talked to a woman
doctor for an hour on Mondays and Thursdays. That helped a
lot: after six months it was cut down to once a week, then
after a while once a month, finally it tailed off altogether at the
end of last year. But if I want to any time, she told me I can
always go back and start seeing her regularly again.

So far there's been no need, as yet. It's been quite close on
several occasions; I've almost felt I couldn't cope any longer,
I'd either have to go back to her or try the other thing again.
I'd say at the moment I've still a long way to go, I'm nothing
like over the hump. If nought was when I tried to kill myself,
and a hundred was if I was normally alive and existing, I'd
place myself at present at around forty. It might get better, it
might get worse; I just can't tell.

I feel it ought to be better than it is, really, in view of the
circumstances. I've been at teacher-training college a year, I've
got a decent grant from the authorities, everything now *should*
be all right. I leave Timmy with Mum during the day, and pick
him up on the way home at the end of the afternoon. I've
made a lot of new friends at college, both boys and girls, and
I'm feeling settled enough to live on my own again, to have a
place of my own. I've even got sensible about birth-control, and
had a coil fitted a few months ago at the clinic.

But these swings of mood, these depressions: they worry
me, they're one of the two major problems in my life. I'd like
to think, or I'd like to hope, they were becoming a bit less
frequent, and a little less long-lasting, each time they occur.
But I just can't tell.

Sometimes when you've come I've been up, and sometimes
down; I think the last three times have all been down, haven't
they? This is really the crucial point, the next day or two: if
I'm not up by the next time you come, then I'm afraid I'll have
to admit I'm not really making progress, you know, at all.

*

Hi, hello, come in. Eaten? If you have I'm warning you, I'll
take it as a direct personal insult, I'll think you don't like my
cooking. Good, sit down then, it won't take long, I open tins
twice as fast as any girl I know. Like the new dress, think it
suits me? My God I went mad, I did honestly, it cost me

nearly ten pounds. Apron, apron, apron, now where the bloody hell has it gone? Yes that's right you are sitting on it too, chuck it over will you, thanks. Daren't get a mark on it, I'm going to a party tomorrow night, it's one of the girls at college's twenty-first. . . .

Well it didn't, so perhaps; and that's about as far as I dare go in saying, just perhaps. One day you know, before long, you never can tell: I might even begin to feel I want to hum to myself once in a while.

Most of all I think if I could I'd like to be able to face very squarely the fact that life can be, and often is, bloody miserable; and to think that I could face it and be sad about it when it is, just in an ordinary sad way like other people manage to do. But I can't, yet. Depression's a hell of a problem when you're depressed.

The other one? Yes that's right, I did didn't I, I did say I had two major problems in life. Well the other one's sex of course. I don't think I'm quite normal about it, at least not from what I gather in conversations I have about it from time to time with other girls. As far as I'm concerned, I like it and I want it; and girls aren't supposed to be like that, or at least if they are they're supposed to pretend that they're not. Only I never know if they really are pretending. Most of the girls I talk to, I don't think they are; I really do think they're not all that keen on it, nothing like I am. One girl at college told me the other day she doesn't even like being kissed.

You once asked me what my idea of a thoroughly enjoyable evening out would be. I think at the time I only told you half of it; I said I'd like to be taken out for a meal and then to a theatre, by a handsome man who'd treat me all evening as though I was a woman—open doors for me, fetch my coat, give me his undivided attention and a bit of flattery, hold my hand a few times, and then make a pass at me in the back of the taxi when he brought me home.

And when I told you, then I laughed and left it at that. But frankly, if he left it at that I'd be very disappointed. I should start worrying there was something wrong with me, that I wasn't pretty or physically attractive I mean, if he politely wished me good night and left me on the doorstep, and wouldn't come in for a coffee or something before he went on home.

I would want him to come in, and within an hour at the very outside I'd want him to be in bed with me and making love to me. I'd want him to stay all night, and keep on waking me up and doing it again: and I'd want to have at least three climaxes with him during the night, and then another last final one before we got up and dressed in the morning.

I'm not saying the going to bed and the love-making would be all that mattered; I'd enjoy all the other part of the evening first. But that would be the rounding off of it, and if it didn't end like that I'd be bitterly disappointed. I'm afraid when I talk to men and listen to them talking to me, I have the utmost difficulty sometimes in paying attention to what they're saying: all I'm really wondering about is what they'd be like in bed if I could get them there, and scheming about how I could find out.

I've been like this ever since I can remember first becoming conscious of being a female, and a desirable object to males. I told you, didn't I, that the first time it happened, with that boy at the holiday camp, I felt I'd been made for it. I like it, I enjoy it, I want it: it's as simple as that.

What's a girl supposed to do if she feels sexy, or is that only allowed for men? I've never seen any point at all in petting and love-making that isn't going to get anywhere. Once it starts, if it doesn't end up with the full thing I get angry and miserable and bad-tempered and depressed. I don't know what this makes me sound like, a sex-maniac or a nymphomaniac: but it just happens to be what I'm like. I suppose it makes me more often at risk in producing illegitimate children too, because I absolutely loathe birth-control. I wish sex could be just simple and easy and natural, that there was no need for preparation in advance or precautions and all the rest of it; to me they detract from all the most pleasant elements about it there are, which are suddenness and unexpectedness and surprise.

Birth-control, if you use it, makes a big difference to men, too. They're completely illogical about it though, of course. They start making passes at you, you go through the formalities of token resistance, and you finally give in. And then usually there comes that moment when just for a second they hesitate: so you say 'It's all right, go on, I've taken precautions, go ahead.'

You can see it flash across their faces, most of them, exactly what they're thinking, clear as daylight: 'Oh—she's that sort of a girl, is she?' In fact it even seems to affect their virility, it throws them right out of their stride. For some reason, they always want to feel they've made a conquest; they don't like it at all, this announcement you're ready for all comers at all times.

That boy Nick, the father of my first child; the phrase he used was 'I suppose you've got yourself pregnant, have you?' I was a lot younger then, I couldn't come back with the proper reply. It's that I hadn't got myself pregnant, because it's impossible; he'd contributed fifty per cent. But a lot of men, and women for that matter, almost always automatically tend to think of it in terms of a girl 'getting herself pregnant'.

Being like this really is a problem I can't resolve. One half of me, the intellectual brainy part of me, tells me I shouldn't be like it, talks to me in terms of not allowing myself to be at the mercy of my feelings, keeping a grip on myself, retaining self-respect and all sorts of clichés like that. But the other half of me knows me for what I am: someone who likes to receive and give attention, and demonstrate it; someone whose sexual feelings and desires are easily aroused, who once she's started on a course of physical contact enjoys it very much, and wants it to go on to what seems its normal and natural conclusion.

It scares me though sometimes, too. Sometimes I can't help wondering if affection's like money, and if you go on handing it out so freely and easily, one day you'll end up bankrupt and without any more to spend.

I know it's promiscuity, or what most people call promiscuity, in the sense that I'm separating sex from the rest of things, I don't have long-lasting and meaningful relationships with men. But that's what I'm like if I'm going to be honest about myself, what's the use of pretending otherwise? Thank you very much, but I don't want to be stuck with one man. I want to pick and choose and have the right to sample those I fancy, with no commitment on either side. After all, it's what most men do, or certainly would like to do if they could. What is it about women that says they've got to be different?

Sometimes I dream of being married, settling down, having a proper home and family. But I know it is a dream; it wouldn't be me. No man would put up for long with a woman who asserted a right to go to bed with any man she chose, if she could get him there, whenever she wanted. That's a prerogative men reserve strictly for themselves.

*

—We've been talking off and on, what, fifteen, eighteen weeks altogether, haven't we? You've seen me depressed, you've seen me happy, you've listened to all my mixed-up confusion and ramblings. I hope sometimes I've been able to talk in a way that made sense and came pretty close to what I meant. But I wonder what kind of a picture you've got at the end of it, how I must appear? Unstable, depressive, schizophrenic, sex-mad, irresponsible, obstinate, stupid? I'm all those things, and a lot of others: only not all the time, and not altogether. I'm a sort of amalgam, with a few good bits as well in between.

I'd say the good bits are probably the ones to do with Timmy. As he gets older, I get older; as he becomes more of a person, so I become more of a person. I find myself getting more involved with him; this is something I've never done before, become involved with another person, I mean. Before, I've always lived inside my own head.

But now I am beginning to start thinking a bit about the future; even to admit there is a future and that I'm going to be part of it. That's something I've never ever been able to do before. Slowly it's beginning to dawn on me there's something more than my own personal future to be thought about too, there's Timmy's as well. A couple of years ago, when I made that second attempt at suicide, I hadn't really accepted his future was my responsibility, because the acceptance of that was something I was trying to get out of.

I'm not saying I still do accept it fully: when I get in a real depression, it goes right out of my head and I don't care. But the depressions are getting just a little bit less frequent, and last just a little less longer each time. And I'm confident enough to have left home again. Mum didn't want me to, but I felt if I was ever going to grow up I had to prove to myself that I could.

I think being at college helps a lot; I don't feel quite so

hemmed in as I used to. I get the opportunity there to talk to other people, read books, stretch my mind and use my brain. Also not having Timmy on top of me all day, with nothing to do but sit and think and worry; now I find when I go to fetch him at the end of the day from Mum's, I really enjoy being able to bring him back here. I enjoy his company, I even make plans for what we're going to do and where we're going to go on little outings at week-ends.

I have a kind of feeling too, though I may be wrong, that in a way this forming of a relationship with him might eventually teach me how to form one with someone else, one that wasn't based just on what I wanted but took account of him as well. Yes, I do mean a man: I'm really a very conventional girl, you know, at heart. Timmy's starting up some very mysterious kinds of maternal feelings in me. I enjoy looking after him and caring for him: and that in turn makes me think one day I might even meet a man who I'd want to look after and care for too.

It's funny, it all seems to be happening back to front, if you know what I mean. Most women marry a man and have a lot of maternal feeling towards him, then they have children and transfer the feeling to them. But I've started with the child and the maternal feeling, and I'm beginning to think it might be possible for me to transfer some of it, if the right man ever comes along, onto him. I think that'll be a few years yet: I'm not going to try and force it, but I am conscious of a few faint stirrings in that direction.

The main immediate problem outside me is still Timmy; how I'm going to cope on my own with bringing him up. By the time he's five or six I'll have qualified from college, and I'll have a job so I'll be able to support us. But I'm not deluding myself by thinking he isn't going to be deprived, because he hasn't got a father or at least a father-figure. I've got to try and work out how best to help him adjust to being illegitimate; and I am working on it, up here in my brain like I always do with problems, but I haven't reached a solution yet. All I'd say to my own credit is that at least I am thinking about it at last.

And perhaps I'm making too much of it; that's always a danger, that you overemphasise something and make it worse than it ought to be by doing so. This is something I've never quite been able to understand; some mothers of illegitimate children don't seem able intellectually to realise the difficulties facing their child in its future, yet somehow they do seem to be able to cope all right: whereas others realise all the problems only too well, yet that doesn't help them, and they can't cope. Me, of course as usual, I want it both ways: I want to understand and cope.

I want to give Timmy some kind of a decent future as a person in his own right, and not grow up into a mother's boy. This means I've got to try and strike a balance in my own personality so I can avoid swamping him with attention and affection, yet give him enough to stop him feeling unloved or unwanted. To do that, I've got to retain my own individuality and personality, yet at the same time not be selfish. That's a hell of a lot to try to achieve really, isn't it, for a little girl?

Oh yes, I am still a little girl, and I don't just mean in height. I've always wanted to be one and I've always wanted to stay one, I never really wanted to grow up, ever. It's so much easier to be a child, you see, nobody makes demands on you; you can get away with things. If you are a child, people are much more tolerant of you.

And my most attractive quality to a lot of men does seem to be this little-girlishness. They like me because I'm small and lively and carefree and happy-go-lucky: or so they think. Then after a while, inevitably, they see the other side of me: either the dreary self-centred depressive, or the flighty promiscuous unfaithful little ... well, it's usually some term of masculine opprobrium.

I used to ask you, and I used to ask myself, which one was the 'real' me? Have I got to face that it's both, that I'm never going to escape the fact that there are two persons living in here, in this shape that from the outside looks as though there's really hardly enough room in it even for one? Or am I really ever going to end up a whole and complete person, who fits neatly into life and is a proper part of it?

Sometimes I think it goes right back to my birth, you know. Because I wasn't expected or intended; I wasn't really meant. It's true, I was a last minute addition to the story of somebody else's life. Perhaps it sounds ridiculous; but I've never been able to rid myself of a feeling it's not just entirely coincidental my initials happen to be 'P.S.'

*

CHAPTER FIVE

SALLY MORRISON

Once I had so little, and now I have so much.

On a blanket spread on the floor by her chair the seven-month fair haired baby in the nappy wriggled and gurgled with pleasure in the sunlight of the summer afternoon, waving arms and legs and kicking bare feet up in the enjoyable air. She lowered her hand, circling it, splaying her fingers to feel the movements and diminutive touches against her palm, and sat smiling out at the blue sky beyond the window with the liquid of tears welling in her eyes.

—I suppose I can't really put it into words at all, she said softly; only that, only that once I had so little, and now I have so much.

*

You said try and keep a sort of diary during the period we're talking, and write down in it whatever I want and whenever I feel like it. In the tape-recorded conversations we do, you guide and I follow, or vice versa; I'm afraid when you come to read it you'll not find this notebook thing very helpful, if you're going to try to use it as well as recordings in building up a picture of me—always providing you can read my untidy scrawling handwriting, for a start, that is, which I very much doubt.

I'm not even sure what sort of thing you want me to put in this. Since you've not given any kind of indication at all, I think I'll just start off with a straightforward description of myself, at least as I see me, that is. When we've finished I'll have to leave it entirely to you to decide whether you want to use any of it or not, or if you think it better just to stick to the recordings. I'm sure I shall do even more rambling about and going off the point in writing than I do in talking. However all I can do is try. I don't quite know where to begin: at the beginning, I suppose.

My name is Sally Morrison. I'm twenty-two and I have two children, a three year old boy called Peter and a baby daughter of seven months whose name is Jemma. I'm not married. I never have been married, and I don't think I ever shall be, and certainly can't ever see myself wanting to be. I live on my own with the children in two rooms which have a connecting kitchen in between, on the ground floor of an old-fashioned semi-detached house in what can't be described as anything more than a small and totally characterless town on the outskirts of London. It's like dozens of others: the sort of place which isn't quite near enough to London to be part of it, and not far enough away to have developed any sort of individuality of its own.

I don't work for my living, not unless you call bringing up two small children working. I certainly often feel it is; but I mean other than that I don't have a job. I live on Social Security Benefit, and have done so for the past three years; it's enough to get by on, but only just. The accommodation I have couldn't exactly be called posh; in fact it's definitely unposh. There isn't a single item of furniture in it that looks anything other than old, worn down and secondhand. Which isn't surprising, because that's exactly what it all is.

What next? Well, after that I suppose I ought to describe what I look like. I've just been and had a careful look at myself in the mirror over the fireplace before trying to do it. I can't think of anything much to put, other than that as far as I can see I'm fairly ordinary in appearance. Rather plump and short, I'd say, about five feet four, and a bit round shouldered because I never stand up straight or sit up straight in a chair; and I've got big feet. Also I have a big nose; at least I think it's big in comparison with the rest of my face, I'm always rather self-conscious about it. My eyes are blue, perhaps greeny-blue would be more accurate. At present my face is covered with freckles: it always is in summer time.

I have fair hair, very long, which comes down to below my shoulders; I can't do anything with it when I've washed it, or before for that matter, so I always wear it parted in the middle and then just leave it hanging down all round my face loose and floppy. It usually looks lank and untidy, as though I don't pay much attention to looking after it apart from washing it twice a week; which is because I don't do anything else but that to it.

Now I've been and had another closer look at my face in the mirror, to see if I can be a bit more specific about it. But I still find it hard to describe, other than by saying I don't think it could be called either particularly pretty or particularly ugly. I can't say more than that it's quite ordinary, apart from the big nose: it's oval-shaped, with a pointed chin and a wide mouth. I never, or hardly ever, wear any make-up on it. Firstly because I usually can't afford to, but also because I can never really be bothered to take the trouble.

To sum up my appearance, then, I'd say I was more or less ordinary looking in nearly every way, and small with short legs. Perhaps in some ways usually a bit boyish in aspect because of my clothing: I nearly always wear cotton shirts or blouses, and jeans, and walk around all day indoors with bare feet. I generally look sloppy, but if I'm going out somewhere special any time, which isn't often, and I feel like making a bit of an effort to improve how I look, which also isn't very often either, I try to tidy up my hair and put on one of my wide selection of dresses, of which at the moment I have two. One is long and a kind of gun-metal grey colour, with a high collar and long sleeves, and it reaches all the way down to my ankles. It has a pattern that looks a bit like big black dragons' tails all over it. The other dress I have is a shorter more summery one of cotton, with wide blue and green stripes.

I remember a few months ago a boy-friend of a girl I know said he thought I looked a bit like a gypsy. I should think that was fairly accurate, except I haven't got a swarthy complexion. I hope he wasn't implying he thought I looked dirty, because I'm not and so I don't think he was. But if he simply meant I usually looked generally untidy, then that would be true as a rule.

Nothing else strikes me as being very important to put down, to complete the physical description. Except perhaps I should add that I've got long fingers with stubby nails on the end of them, and which now and again I try to stop biting but don't usually succeed in keeping it up for long.

That's just about everything I can think of to describe what I look like, or think I look like. As far as what I'm actually like as a person is concerned, rather than my appearance, of course that's something that's much more difficult to try to write about. I am leaving that to you to convey in the transcriptions of the tape-recordings of the conversations that we have. I couldn't do it myself in writing like this in a notebook.

As you'll have noticed, I always need some sort of lead from you before I can get going.

*

—Do you remember any details of what the cat was like, the one you were holding in your arms and stroking the night you told me about last time, when you were sitting up in bed and your mother came up to your bedroom and told you the truth?

—No, only that it was big and fluffy, with long silvery-grey hair and yellow eyes, and that it was called 'Smokey'. Oh and I have a kind of dim recollection too that she might have given it me as a present for my ninth birthday which was a few weeks before.

—Did she use that actual word?

—Illegitimate, you mean? No I shouldn't think so; I don't think at that age I'd have known what it meant even if she had. It was probably more along the lines of saying something like I was old enough to be told now that my father hadn't really been killed in the war as she'd always said up till then; he was still alive, but she didn't know where he was and she hadn't ever been married to him. She explained that he'd been married all the time to somebody else, and she thought by then he was probably back in his home country which was Canada. She'd never seen him since before I was born, and he didn't know anything about me. I was getting quite good at arithmetic in school by that age, which is why I should think she decided to tell me then. She knew it wasn't going to be long before I could work out for myself that by the time I was born, the war had already been finished for several years.

I definitely didn't feel at all upset about it. In fact I think I must have felt rather proud, as though it made me someone more like everyone else, because I remember her ticking me off a few days later for telling all my friends at the school in the village about it. I was going round saying to everyone that my daddy wasn't really dead at all, he was still alive and lived in Canada and wasn't married to my mummy. I think possibly it was me doing that which led to our leaving the village soon afterwards, and coming up to live in furnished rooms in different places in London. Up till that time she'd been living quietly with her mother and father in the village, where they had the little grocer's shop. I suppose she wasn't able then to keep up her pose as a widow any longer, when I went round telling everyone about it.

No honestly it's never bothered me at all, at least not so far as I'm aware. All the books I've ever come across which deal with the subject say illegitimate children always go through a stage at some time of building up a kind of dream picture of their fathers, and often in adolescence they start wanting to try and find them. But I never have, not on any kind of conscious level anyway. I've never had fantasies about him or even felt the faintest desire to meet him and see what he looks like. I think it must be because up till the age of nine I'd always thought of him as completely dead. When she told me he wasn't, I suppose I must have preferred to keep him that way in my mind. He was a dead person, somebody who didn't exist. I still do think of him, I always have thought of him like that, not ever thought about him as a living being at all.

When my mother moved up to London with me to live on our own, I think the first job she got for herself was as a shop assistant in one of the big stores in Oxford Street. Whatever it was, I know it didn't last very long. She had a whole succession of different jobs, usually in shops and offices, once or twice as a waitress I think. I don't exactly know why she was always changing, but I should imagine if she was like then what she's like now, very neurotic and difficult to get on with, she wouldn't have been able to stay anywhere for more than a few months without quarrelling with the people she worked with.

My main recollection is the result, that for about three or four years we were always changing the place we lived in. I suppose usually it was because she had money difficulties over the rent, or wanted to be near whatever new work she was doing. In turn that meant I was perpetually changing schools; North London, South London, West London, all over. I was never at one long enough either to make any friends, or to make much kind of progress in education. God I hated it; I remember all that as a terribly unhappy period indeed in my life. I'd been very happy as a small child. I'd liked the country life in the village, and I'd been very fond of my grandparents. I hated my mother for taking me away from it, and I resented that it was all apparently finished and done with for ever, which it was.

I often asked her, but she'd never tell me exactly why we couldn't go back. But putting two and two together now, I think it can't just have been my revealing that she wasn't married which was the only cause of us having to leave the village. There must have been more to it than that. As far as I know she hasn't been back to see her parents ever since, and I've certainly lost all contact with them myself. The last time I asked her, which was a few years ago now, she said she couldn't even remember the name of the village. I don't believe her, and so I presume they must have had a very big row indeed about something, and have made an absolutely irreparable break.

I've never asked her any more details about it, and quite honestly I don't think there's any chance I ever will. She and I are not on good terms at all now, and hardly see each other. I've grown up and got children of my own, and as she gets older we seem to have drifted further and further apart. We're totally unlike each other, we don't get on, and we don't have any interests in common whatsoever. I don't like her as a person, I never have, and I don't really want to try any more. Whenever I do go and see her I take the children over with me but she's not at all interested in them. And we always start arguing within the first quarter of an hour, so I don't make the effort to trail all the way over to the other side of London these days. Sometimes I have slight pangs of conscience, I feel I ought to have one more try at getting on with her. But I'm afraid I've reached the stage of having to admit to myself that, much as I regret it for the children's sake, because after all she is their grandma, things between us will never be any better, and can only get worse.

It's not a nice thing to say about your own mother, but I feel now she's almost like a complete stranger. Though I think it's inevitable this would have happened anyway, I mean in whatever direction either of our lives had developed. In fact, now I come to think about it and start looking back at it from a distance, I'm beginning to understand a lot of things much more clearly than I did, or could be expected to, as a child.

I mean for instance, well, like my whole parental relationship business. Earlier on, when I was talking about my lack of any strong conscious feelings concerning not having a father, I think it wasn't only because of a kind of psychological blocking-off. You see, I did have at least a very acceptable father substitute in my grandpa; I always felt very close to him as a child, even though he was quite an elderly man. He was always extremely nice and jolly and affectionate, he was for ever picking me up and sitting me on his knee and cuddling me. So was my grandma, she was very much the same sort of person; she gave me a lot of attention and care and affection. And I never remember my mother doing any of these things at all.

I think what I'm trying to say is that as a child both my grandparents, my grandpa and my grandma, became substitute parents. When my mother took me away from them and the village and brought me up to London with her she made a mistake. She should have left me there. I had very strong feelings of resentment towards her about it, and even now I still have.

She had strong feelings of resentment towards me too, and there was no doubt about them, she always made them very plain. I remember that as I got older and into my early teens she was always telling me whenever we had rows, which was pretty often, that I wasn't sufficiently grateful to her for all she'd done and been through because of me. She was quite explicit about it, about not wanting me or ever having wanted me, I mean. She used to shout and scream at me for being dirty and untidy, and not making any effort to do homework at the different schools I went to. And it always ended with her telling me that if it hadn't been for me she could have found somebody nice to marry her, instead of having to go on like she was, working to provide for me, and all the rest of it.

I suppose with a bit of an effort I can look back with a certain amount of detachment now, and feel sorry for her. I realise she must have had a very hard struggle, and hadn't exactly been born with the right sort of temperament for it. But of course I didn't see it like that then, as an adolescent girl. I reacted by hating her deeply for taking me away from a place and people where I'd spent all my childhood and been happy.

I used to play truant from school an awful lot because she was out at work, and I spent my time wandering round the streets; I suppose the only surprising thing is I never came to much harm and didn't get into any kind of trouble. But it did make me into a very lone-wolf kind of person.

At week-ends I'd knock about in cafés and at street corners with other young people of around my own age, some of whom were pretty rough types. By the time I was fourteen I was hardly ever going to school any more. I used to spend days on end hitching long rides all over the country on lorries, usually with another girl-friend or two. I was big for my age, very much an old shirt and jeans sort of girl even then, like I am now. I suppose I must have looked at least about seventeen or eighteen, so nobody ever asked me why I wasn't still at school. My mother used to complain about it, but did nothing more than drop dark hints about me coming to a bad end or getting into trouble. I took it at that time she meant becoming involved in crime or something of that sort, but I never did. I always thought she was making a lot of fuss about nothing, and didn't understand all I was interested in was freedom, which to me simply meant being away from her and leading my own life.

To her, to her generation I mean, the phrase actually meant becoming pregnant I suppose, like she'd done. It's funny it never struck me at the time, that that was what she was referring to. I think it didn't strike me because there was never any question of it. I was a virgin, I'd had no experience of sex at all ever, and I always resisted any attempts made on my virtue that some men who gave me lifts occasionally tried with me from time to time, simply because I wasn't interested.

It might sound strange, but I usually hitched in lorries and lorry-drivers were always absolutely safe. I can't ever remember a single one who made any kind of advance or suggestion to me at all. Quite the worst of the lot without any doubt were middle-aged commercial travellers in cars, so I always tried to avoid them. You knew if it was one of those who offered you a lift, the majority would invariably try and bring the conversation round to the subject of where you were going to sleep that night. They'd say the back seat of their car was very comfortable, they often slept in it themselves if they couldn't find anywhere, all that sort of thing.

Or even if it was in the middle of the day, they'd start telling you they'd plenty of free time, how would it be if they forgot work for the afternoon and took you out for a drive in the country; the countryside was always very nice round there, whatever part of the world they happened to be in. They hardly ever varied, they all made what I suppose they thought were original and subtle approaches of that kind.

Oh and God they were always for ever trying to put one hand on your knee while they were driving, or get their arm round your shoulder; to demonstrate what good drivers they were I suppose, how they could manipulate their car one-handed. Sometimes I used to think there must be a special training-school for them somewhere.

Even though I can laugh about it while I'm telling you, I've always had an absolute horror of commercial travellers ever since. Whenever I even hear the words, I get a nasty taste in my mouth. It's ridiculous, obviously they can't possibly all be the same, but I must have just been unlucky with the ones I always met. As a young girl I classified them without exception as dirty old men, or at least as dirty middle-aged men. Oh and of course too there was always the what's-a-pretty-young-girl-like-you-doing-travelling-around-on-her-own line that went with it, and the same old air of wanting to sell me seduction wrapped up as though it was fatherly protectiveness.

I wasn't anti-men or anti-sex or anything like that. I suppose that I simply wasn't old enough to be really very aware of it or interested in it. I didn't find I had to conquer any strong feelings of nausea or reaction against it later on when I first went to bed with a boy. But even now, though I know it's ridiculous, the mere mention of commercial travellers still gives me a slightly crawly sort of feeling, and this is eight years and two babies afterwards. I know if I were ever to think of getting married later on in life to someone who had a steady job, I should put travellers absolutely at the bottom of the list of possible categories of suitable husband.

Anyway that's all rather off the point. At least you can tell from how long I've gone on about it, though, how strong my feelings about them as a species are, can't you? There must have been some nice ones, God knows there are enough of them. But perhaps the nice ones are those who get on with their jobs and don't stop and offer lifts to young girls.

Well, to get back to the main thread of my life story. I must have spent two or three years between the ages of fourteen and seventeen leading that sort of wandering life, living with my mother at whatever address she happened to be at in London, but spending as much time as I could travelling round and keeping away from her. I had a huge variety of different jobs to keep myself alive. Once I worked for a time with a travelling circus, not as a performer of course but looking after the animals. Another time I had a job for a few months on a farm, in fact I had several jobs of that sort; casual work, pea-picking and so on, and at one they had a vacancy for a more permanent job in a kind of dairy which was attached to the farm, where I stayed for about three months or more.

I did all kinds of other things too. I worked in the hop-fields, at hay-making, potato-picking—anything at all that was an outdoor job so I could be out in the country. I was never much of a town girl. Then I was a sort of domestic help for a while to a couple who had a dog-breeding establishment. I went for a job with the dogs because I liked animals, and ended up spending my time mostly looking after their two small kids while they went off to exhibitions and shows. They were a very nice couple, and very good to me. The only thing wrong with the work in those days was that I preferred animals to children. I'd much sooner have helped them with the dogs, and after about six months with them there I decided to give up and come back to London.

By then I was certain I didn't want to live with my mother at all any more. I kept in touch with her but lived as far away as possible, right over the other side of London, and got myself a small furnished room. I was walking down a street one day and saw a funny little secondhand bookshop-cum-picture dealer, with a handwritten notice on a postcard in the window, saying it wanted an assistant. Just on the off-chance I thought I'd go in and try my luck. There was a little wizened old man inside, he was very sweet actually; he had a funny croaky voice so I could hardly tell what he was saying.

The wage he was offering was abysmal, I think it was only about four or five pounds a week, which is why I suppose he couldn't get anybody. When I asked him if I'd do, he said yes yes I was just the sort of person he was looking for, if I wanted I could start there and then straight away. I'd hardly been in the shop ten minutes before he'd put his coat and hat and muffler on, and said he'd leave me in charge, he had to go out to buy a few things at an auction sale, and then off he went.

The shop was very poky and dirty, full of old pictures and antiquated books, so he wasn't really taking much of a risk with me: there wasn't a thing of any value at all there. It was in a back street, there were no passing customers and so he hardly ever did any business. I should think he must have been very hard put to it, in view of how little money he actually took in a week, even to pay my wages. But he did, and that was all that mattered as far as I was concerned. What I earned just about covered my rent, and left me sufficient over to buy enough food to keep myself alive.

I wasn't exactly worked to death. Nobody ever came into the shop, and the old man was always out rummaging round sale-rooms for things to sell and make a few shillings profit on. I used to spend most of my time just sitting there reading. The books weren't exactly up-to-date literature or the latest best sellers, but having nothing much else to do I ploughed through all sorts of incredible things like the Works of Sir Walter Scott, old sets of Dickens, ancient encyclopaedias which described things like the very latest steam-railway engines, and had pictures of trams in them, and all sorts of things like that. I got quite fascinated with them after a time; and at least it started me off reading, which I'd never done much of before. I've always been very keen on it ever since, though now my taste in subjects has got a bit wider and more up to date.

I must have been there about a year or perhaps a bit more, and on the whole I was quite happy. I lost a lot of my restless-ness and desire to be perpetually travelling about. After a time I found there was a youth club near by attached to a church; and even though I was no more a church-goer or religious in any way than I am now, they let me join. It was all very innocent and innocuous, just a record-player and cups of coffee three nights a week. But there were an incredible number of young people there, who seemed to come from all over the place. Some were locals, but others came from miles away: I never knew why, perhaps it was the only place of its kind in that area of London.

By then I'd be over seventeen, perhaps nearly eighteen. One of the boys who used to come to the church youth club regularly was a chap whose name was Steve, who worked in a local photographer's shop. He was about a couple of years older than me, originally he came from somewhere up in the north of England I think, and he was living on his own in digs. I believe both his parents were dead, and he didn't seem to have any brothers or sisters, or relatives of any kind.

He was quite good-looking, very quiet and shy, and rather thin and tall. In his lunch-hour he sometimes used to come round to the shop where I was working, and bring sandwiches for both of us; I'd make us a mug of coffee each, and we used to sit and chat. It wasn't about anything much, but somehow we just seemed to get on well.

We never went out together, and apart from seeing each other at the shop, the only other place we met was three times a week at the youth club. One day he said very casually he didn't like being in digs much and had found a new place to live, which was a furnished bed-sitter. Only it was a double room, he said, and he couldn't afford it on his own, so he was looking for somebody to share it with him.

I forget whether it was he who asked me, or whether it was me who offered. Anyway it seemed quite natural, the idea of us living together I mean. By then we really were on very friendly terms with each other, though not on any sexual basis, much more like a sort of brother and sister feeling. So we agreed that's what we'd do, and we agreed too it was obvious that we'd have to pretend we were married.

I don't honestly think we were in love with each other then. But I suppose it was inevitable that after living together for a few weeks we should start to be; and we did. There was no sudden dawning of overwhelming physical desire, it just kind of came slowly and naturally that we started sleeping together, and living really as though we were married. I did like Steve very much indeed, in fact I got fonder and fonder of him until I was fairly hopelessly in love with him. And I should think he felt something like the same kind of feeling developing inside him towards me, at the beginning.

We were really very happy for quite a long time, it must have been for nearly a year. I suppose you can't love somebody though without getting involved in all sorts of other deep feelings and emotions too. I think what I'm trying to say is that the more we loved each other, the more we started to quarrel as well. Until by the end of twelve months it had become a very tempestuous affaire, violent love-making followed by terrible rows followed by passionate making things up again. When we first met and began to get to know each other, we were both fairly placid and easy-going sort of characters, which is what attracted us and brought us together. But when we became lovers we had an increasingly bad effect on each other, somehow it brought out the worst in both of us.

Finally we decided to split up: we realised it was impossible for either of us to go on as we were doing, and so I left. We separated quite amicably, or at least we pretended to be friendly and sensible about it; though I think in fact by then we both absolutely hated the sight of each other.

I'd never used any sort of birth-control at all, and all the time we'd been together we must have been lucky that nothing happened. So it was very ironic that two months after we'd separated I discovered I was pregnant. I knew it'd be hopeless to even consider the idea of ever living with Steve again; and anyway I'd heard he was already by then living with another girl.

I stayed on at the shop for about three or four months while I tried to think what to do. The idea of abortion never crossed my mind, nor did any thoughts of having the child and then having it adopted. I knew definitely I wanted to have it and keep it, if I could find some way of doing it. I went to see my mother once or twice, but I didn't tell her I was pregnant. I think I had the idea vaguely in my mind that it might be possible to go back and live with her. But every time I saw her we started having a row as usual, so I knew there was no hope of that working out.

The only real friends I had were the couple I'd worked for the year before, the dog-breeders. I hadn't left them as a result of a row or anything, it'd all been on good terms. We'd kept in contact with fairly regular letters ever since, so I decided the only thing to do was to write and tell them what had happened. I said I was pregnant, but I wanted to have the baby and keep it; and I asked them would they consider having me back to live with them until after I'd had it.

They were absolutely sweet and wrote back at once to say I could go there. In fact I think it was within a couple of days the husband came up to London in his car to fetch me. We had an arrangement that I'd go on looking after their children for as long as I could in exchange for my keep and a bit of pocket money; and after I'd had the baby, we'd review the situation to see what adjustments or alternatives needed to be made.

I was nineteen when Peter was born. At that stage I thought it only right to tell Steve, so I wrote to him and said I'd had a son and I was calling him Peter, which was Steve's other Christian name. I didn't say in the letter that he was the father. It never crossed my mind anything so obvious needed saying, and also I thought he might construe it as a kind of preamble to a demand for money, which it certainly wasn't going to be. I was very shocked and hurt when about a couple of weeks later I got a letter back, not from Steve but from his girl-friend whose name I think was Elizabeth, saying very pointedly that Steve had told her all about me. She wrote she was glad to hear both me and the baby were well, and she wished us both good luck in the future.

There was a distinct air of suggestion in the way she phrased the whole letter that in view of what she'd heard about me from Steve, she wasn't at all surprised to know I'd had an illegitimate child. Whatever he'd said to her must obviously have painted a picture of me as some kind of promiscuous tart. I suppose he must have done it to protect himself, I imagine. For a day or two I felt so angry about it I really did feel like writing straight back and pointing out what was the absolute truth, which was that I'd never been to bed with anyone else in my life. But then I thought there was simply no point in it: obviously he'd fabricated the whole account of our relationship, and would only flatly deny that Peter was his. In a day or two I calmed down, and so I didn't even bother to reply.

Of course my reaction was to feel very strongly indeed, if that was the way he wanted it then that was the way it would be. He'd made it quite plain he didn't want to have anything to do with Peter either then or in the future, and he was taking up the firm line he wasn't his. As far as I was concerned, all right then, he wasn't: Peter had nothing to do with Steve. He was entirely mine, and nobody else's. That was how I thought about him then, and how I always have thought about him ever since. And I know it's how I shall think about him always in the future.

I stayed on at the dog-breeder friends' place, and it was at least six months before I even got round to writing to tell my mother I'd had Peter. Long before that time I'd come to feel she was almost a total stranger, so I'd really got nothing to do with her at all. As she didn't write back, presumably she must have felt the same. So by the time I was twenty, the only person in the world who meant anything at all to me, or who I meant anything to myself, was Peter.

*

I really did intend last night to make a big effort at getting something more written down in this notebook. I got Jemma off to sleep at about half-past six, then I played with Peter for a while and read him a story after I'd got him into bed. Much to my surprise he didn't make his usual endless succession of excuses for getting up again for drinks of water or doing wee-wee, but instead he snuggled down happily in his cot and went to sleep more or less straight away.

Then I made myself a boiled egg and a slice of toast and a mug of coffee, and settled down to write here at the kitchen table. Before I'd even begun, Jemma woke up and started crying, I think because it was a rather hot sultry evening. I walked around with her for a bit and nursed her back to sleep; but every time I tried to put her back in her cot she woke up again. Eventually I put her in the one place where she always sleeps perfectly happily, which is in my bed.

By that time Peter had woken up again himself, and as soon as he heard me putting Jemma in my bed he started to create too, because he was feeling jealous I suppose. He simply wouldn't stay in his cot or even try to go back to sleep unless I put him in my bed as well. Which I did, with the obvious disastrous results—he started giggling and playing about under the bed-clothes and calling out to me all the time, until he'd woken Jemma up and she then joined in with him at making a racket.

Nothing would do for either of them, until I had to lie down on the bed and pretend we were all going to sleep. At least that was my intention, I thought when they'd both gone off I'd slip

out again. But the next thing I knew after that was Peter push-
ing me in the back saying he was hungry and wanted his breakfast. When I looked at the clock I saw it was seven o'clock this
morning. So much for my good intentions.

I do find myself getting very tired at the end of the day,
trying to cope with two small children. Sometimes I wonder if
I've done the right thing in having them. Then I tell myself it's
a bit late to start wondering that, because I've already done it
and don't have any choice but to get on with it. I suppose I
shall survive. After all, I can't be the first woman who's ever
been in the position of trying to bring up children on her own,
and I don't suppose I'll be the last.

But it is at times like that when I really do feel the desire to
have someone else to share the burden of them with. That's a
very selfish attitude, I suppose. I mean if the only time I regret
not having someone else here, is for them to share the difficulties. Logically someone else would have just as much right to
share the pleasures and happiness of having the children as
well, but at those times the idea never enters my head, I'm
perfectly content on my own. Which as I say is very selfish of
me, as well as being illogical.

All this isn't what I was intending to write about anyway, as
I'm sure it'll come up in conversation as we go along. If it
does, I hope I'm able to sort out my thoughts a bit better in
talking than I can in writing. What I was really intending to do
instead was try and write some more description of me and my
surroundings.

Turning back the pages I see last time I fairly well covered,
as well as I'm able to anyway, what I looked like as a person.
What I'll try and do now is put down a few more details of my
surroundings. All I've written so far is that I live in two furnished rooms, or more correctly poorly-furnished rooms, with a
kitchen in between them. What I haven't tried to describe yet is
anything about what they contain, or how they look.

Well they look, and are, like me: which is thoroughly untidy. I should think 'higgledy-piggledy' would be a good general term to start off with. All the furniture is large and old
and ugly, because I've bought it at secondhand shops or junk
shops or auction sales. I know this is all very fashionable and
trendy now. In fact only the other day I saw in a newspaper
somebody had opened a big secondhand furniture shop in

London called 'Junk City'. But I don't think any of this furniture would ever qualify for that standard. It's all throw-outs that people must have been absolutely desperate to get rid of, otherwise they wouldn't have been selling for the prices I paid for them.

My bed, which is a rickety old divan, cost me ten shillings; Peter's drop-side cot and Jemma's folding carrycot cost me five shillings each. The bedroom floor doesn't have a carpet, and its curtains are made out of an old length of material a vaguely-related cousin friend gave me last year. In the kitchen where I'm sitting there are numerous old pots and pans I pick up from time to time for sixpence or a shilling each at jumble sales. This wobbly table which I'm now writing on I got for nothing from the woman who lives in the house next door, who said she never used it (which doesn't surprise me). Also in this room are two chairs which I bought at jumble sales, and an old gas cooker which was here when I arrived.

I haven't got a refrigerator. But I have got a washing-machine, which is essential for the children's clothes. I don't know how long it will last: I bought it secondhand of course. It was standing on the pavement outside an ironmonger's shop marked 'Bargain, £2'. I'm not so sure now that it was, because it makes a terrible rattling noise and shoots out water in all directions when it's being used. I've also got an ironing-board (secondhand) and an electric iron (jumble sale). What I haven't got, but would very much like, is a high chair for Peter to sit in now he's getting bigger. I expect I'll see one before long somewhere; I never pass any kind of junk shop without going in to see if they've got anything cheap which I need or could put to good use.

I've now moved into what I'll very grandly call the sitting-room, and will make an attempt at describing it. I look round, and what I see everywhere can be summed up in one word: chaos. Starting from the door and working round the walls; first of all there's a long wooden bookshelf absolutely crammed with books, either cheap paper-back editions or secondhand ones. I'm an inveterate reader (when I'm not too tired), and I read nearly everything I can lay my hands on, even though I can't afford to spend money on books and shouldn't, and know I'm being terribly extravagant. The subjects I'm chiefly interested in are sociology and social history and politics, and

the books are things like *The Family Life Of Old People,
Social Structure and Group Dynamics,* George Orwell's
novels, *The Elements of Political Theory,* and so on. Hardly
any fiction.

I have a vague idea, though so far it is only an idea and not
much more, that when the children are old enough to go to
nursery-school I might start trying to get down to some study-
ing, and do something about improving my education, like
trying to pass some exams. I really would like to have some
kind of intellectual life for myself in the future rather than just
sitting around and vegetating. At the present time I don't have
much alternative, but I've no intention of opting out of society
or life in general. Perhaps one day in the not too distant future
I might be able to take a more direct and active interest. And if
I'm going to be honest about it and it doesn't sound too arro-
gant I'd like to try and contribute something else to it besides
two children.

What it ever could be, I don't yet know. Only that I would
like it to be something of value, perhaps some kind of social
service work if they'd ever let someone like me into it, and I
could ever get the necessary qualifications. Or some kind of
research work or teaching, anything that had some kind of
value not just for me but to others as well. All this is pie-in-the-
sky at the moment, for the next few years at least. I know I
shall not be content though, when the children start getting
older, just to sit back and be sorry for myself, and go around
with a chip on my shoulder about life having given me a raw
deal. That's one of the things I always most disliked about my
mother, that she did and still does. After all I chose my own
way of life and I certainly don't feel bitter about it.

Hell, this is supposed to be a description of the room. Now
it's nearly midnight and I'm sitting here yawning my head off.
But if I don't finish it I shall lose the impetus. I'll do it as a
kind of shorthand, stop trying to write sentences, just put
down a list of words of what I can see.

Books. Everywhere, along the mantelpiece as well as on the
shelves. Piles of newspapers and magazines, that ought to have
been thrown away long ago, Sunday newspaper colour supple-
ments, the *New Statesman, New Society* (two other terrible
extravagances). Old record player that doesn't work. Two
Aubrey Beardsley prints on wall, present from friend for birth-

day. Reproduction of poster of pop art. Modern paintings calendar, Monets, Matisses, post-Impressionists etc. (Last year's, but still keep because like pictures.) Toys, motor-cars, jigsaw puzzles, building bricks, plastic fire-engine. Pile of baby's nappies (ought to be in bedroom). Big old dining-room table covered with sheets of plain white paper, pots of paint so Peter can do finger-painting (and me too), tins with plasticine in, old scraps of coloured paper to make patterns with, letter-shapes alphabet in cardboard for Peter (homemade), old settee piled up with more books and magazines, tatty old table lamp, vase with dead flowers in (must empty), hair-dryer (broken, needs mending), half cut out material of shirt-type blouse trying to make (been there ages), two second-hand men's cotton vests with buttons, bought last week jumble sale, going to try and tie-dye. Not yet washed-up coffee mug on floor. Carpet on floor has holes in, cost ten shillings at jumble s. Horrible cheap plaster of paris painted cat Peter insisted buying for sixpence in junk shop. Mending-basket on floor under table overflowing children's clothes. Too tired do any more now, but go back to what said at beginning, which is general impression chaos and very untidy. End.

*

—Your feelings about Peter being yours and nobody else's.

—Oh yes that was it wasn't it, yes I remember. It must have sounded very selfish of me to say that. I am a rather selfish sort of person, I think. But I don't see how in those circumstances I had much option, after Steve had made it so clear he didn't want to know. It's a dangerous sort of attitude for any woman to have about her child, though, to look upon it as her own personal private property. Dangerous for the child, I mean, which is why later on I tried to do something to counteract it. However I'll tell you what happened in between before I did that, shall I? Sorry, do forgive me keeping on yawning.

By the time Peter was six months old, my position as a sort of nanny and domestic help to those friends I was living with was becoming very unsatisfactory on both sides. I mean God, you've only got to look at this room haven't you, to see I could never be exactly a howling success at housework and keeping things tidy. At that place I was even less use with a baby of my own than I'd been when I was first there.

I began to feel, and I know they must have felt so too, though they were always nice and didn't say anything about it, that really what it amounted to was my living on their charity and kindness of heart. They hadn't a lot of money, her health wasn't very good; all the work with the dogs, travelling, kennel-keeping, showing and all the rest of it, as well as having two children of her own plus me there as well with my baby, well it was all becoming too much for them. I can't say I was absolutely astonished when they told me they'd decided to sell the place and go and live somewhere else. The husband was going back to his old job that he'd been doing before, he was a qualified quantity surveyor.

I felt it was up to me then: to start trying to build up a life of my own and stand on my own feet, especially now I had the responsibility of Peter. I wouldn't say it was entirely due to moral principles that I decided it, because I think my own natural laziness and disinclination to work came into it as well; but I came to the conclusion a young baby really did need to be with its mother all the time, so I wasn't going to attempt to get a job and put him in someone else's care while I went out and earned a living.

I made enquiries from the Social Security people and worked out that if you didn't have any fancy ideas about high standards of living, which I haven't, it would be just possible to get by and have enough to live on for yourself and your child on National Assistance. I knew a girl who was living in this area, so I wrote and asked her if she thought there was any chance of my finding somewhere on my own to live. She wrote back and said the best thing to do was to come up and stay with her and her husband for a few weeks, and have a look round.

It was very decent of them, because they only had a very small flat; but they put up with me until I found this place. It took much longer than I ever thought it would, nearly three months, but of course finding cheap accommodation isn't easy, especially if you've got to do it trailing everywhere with a baby in a pram. I looked at dozens of places; but they were all either too expensive, or they suddenly and mysteriously had become taken by somebody else the day before, as soon as the agent or owner started enquiring about my husband and I said flatly that I wasn't married.

I wouldn't call this place exactly palatial, and of course I'd much sooner it was either near to London or right out in the country. But it was the best I could find at the time, and I know I was lucky even to get anywhere at all. Oh and in the end I had to lie, by the way, and say I was separated from my husband and in the process of getting a divorce; otherwise I probably wouldn't have got it. I don't wear a wedding-ring and never have, so I doubt if they really believed me, but I suppose they felt I was at least making some attempt at keeping up convention. What they must think now I've had Jemma I can't imagine. Anyway nothing's been said so far, the landlord has an agent who comes round once a month to collect the rent. And so long as that's paid I don't think he's much interested in anything else.

I've been here now nearly two and a half years. Of course I'm always telling myself I really ought to get somewhere a bit less dreary, but I haven't got round to making any serious attempts at doing something about it. I think the longer I stay here the more difficult I shall find it to move away, because I've got quite a few friends now who live around this area, and I would miss them.

Friendships are always something I seem to have been quite lucky about since I've got older. I've got five or six really good friends, all more or less of my own age. There's Alan and Mary, who are a young married couple who live down the road; he's a school-teacher and they've one small child of their own who's the same age as Peter and they often play together. Then there's Sheila and Barbara, they're two girls who share a flat and work up in London in offices in the City. Other close friends are a girl called Margaret who works in an art shop, she gave me those prints up there, and her boy-friend whose name is Stuart and he works as a technician in a television studio. And there's Ron and George, two very nice queers who run a male boutique together, they live quite near; and Robert and Anne, a slightly older married couple who have a card-shop in the town ... all in all there's quite a lot of people I know and am friendly with. The only difficulty is it does get a bit embarrassing sometimes, when they invite me round to their homes for meals with my children, and I can't really do much in the way of returning their hospitality.

I'm certainly not lonely, there always seems to be someone popping in and out nearly every day somehow. Oh and of course Malcolm comes round quite a lot, I see him about three times a week; though I think it'd be truer to say now he comes primarily to see Jemma more than to see me, since she's his daughter.

He's a lot younger than me, by which I mean nearly four years; he's not nineteen yet. When we first met in fact he was still at school.

As I said earlier on, by the time Peter was a year old I was very conscious of the inherent dangers to him in the situation of being an only child and having only one parent. I was in exactly the same position myself in childhood, but at least I did have some kind of substitutes in my grandparents. With Peter too there was the additional complication that he was a boy, and I didn't want him to grow up in an atmosphere of close single relationship to and with his mother, without anyone else in the picture at all.

So from that time on, I always intended to have one other child at least, if not possibly three altogether. Though that's something I haven't made up my mind about one way or the other yet. As it is now, with Jemma still very much an infant, and both of them very demanding and tiring, the mere idea seems too awful to contemplate; but as she gets older no doubt I shall feel up to giving it a bit more rational thought.

When I'd settled in here and become more confident about my ability actually to make a go of things with Peter, I decided the time had come to start looking for someone to have another child by. I suppose this can't very well sound anything else but cold and calculating; and I suppose by only looking at it one way there's no escaping the truth that it is. I wouldn't want to try to pretend, either, that I had Jemma purely and simply for Peter's benefit, because I didn't; I enjoy her very much myself, I like babies, I like being a mother.

What I don't like, and wouldn't like, is to be somebody's wife, or at least not yet. Possibly I might change my mind when I'm older, and if I ever met somebody I fell in love with and who'd take me on with two children of my own already, I might consider it. But as I am at the moment, and I can only talk as I am and as I feel now, I really don't want to have to share my life with anybody else except my children. I simply don't think I could.

Which means that I don't want to share them, my children, with anybody else either. And that I regard them as *my* children and in no way part of, or belonging to, anyone else at all. Perhaps this is due to the kick in the teeth I got from Steve when it was made so clear to me Peter was mine. But I think that's not entirely true, because I'd already fallen out of love with Steve before Peter was born; even if he had wanted to come back with me and share him, I'm certain I wouldn't have agreed.

However, to get back to Jemma and Malcolm. Having made up my mind I wanted to have another child for both my own benefit and Peter's, I began to keep my eyes open for someone suitable to father it. I drew up a kind of list of qualifications in my mind. In the first place, it couldn't be a man who was already married, because I'd no desire to seduce somebody else's husband, with all the complications that might lead to. Secondly I felt it would have to be somebody reasonably near my own age; also it had to be someone I liked and felt a bit physically attracted to, because I didn't want it just to be a casual pick-up or a one night stand affair purely and simply to get myself pregnant.

I think I felt also it would have to be somebody I was reasonably friendly with and knew quite well, because it would involve more than just a sexual relationship. I hoped for the child's sake I could remain on fairly good terms with its father in the future, and not end in the same sort of situation I'd had to face with Peter. So whereas it's true to say to a certain extent I did sort out someone I thought would be right, on the other hand I didn't go as far as being predatory and actually going out hunting. I just waited for a suitable person to turn up.

Malcolm, I realise now, wasn't at all right. Perhaps I'm deceiving myself, and always was, in thinking there ever could be any such person. I think the main fault was and still is that he's too young to cope with it emotionally. At the moment even though he does come round two or three times a week we don't get on at all well, and sometimes we hardly even speak. In all these calculations you see, I'd overlooked one factor; which was that he might fall, as indeed he did fall and still is,

in love with me. This is something I feel rather guilty and
unhappy about; it's what I meant when I said he was not
emotionally old enough for the situation. And I know this is
fundamentally my fault for involving him in it, not his own.

I met him one night round at Robert and Anne's house; I
think he's Robert's sister-in-law's nephew or some kind of
vague relation to them like that. I'd only gone round to see
them briefly, to take back a book I'd borrowed I think. Malcolm was there, and said he'd walk back here with me on his
way home. I asked him in for a cup of coffee and we had a
chat; he left after about half an hour on that occasion and I
never really thought any more about him.

A few days later I met him while I was out shopping, when
we both happened to be looking round the bookshop in the
town. Again he said he'd walk back with me, again he came in
for a cup of tea or coffee, and again he didn't stop very long. I
think the next thing that happened was he turned up here one
evening on his own; we had a long talk about books and about
his 'A' level exam, his hopes of a future career as a journalist
and things like that. Then he took to dropping in quite often
from then onwards, sometimes in the afternoons on his way
home from school and other times in the evenings.

I don't think I can escape it, I did seduce him: though of
course I let him think it was him who was seducing me. He
was really very sweet, he was an absolute virgin and had never
made love properly to a girl before. I liked it when we made
love, and I really was very fond of him indeed. He was absolutely appalled the day I told him I was pregnant, and he
became very public schoolboyish about it, saying he'd do the
right thing by me, he'd marry me straight away. Oh dear, I
really shouldn't smile about it should I, but I can't help it when
I think about it; the absolutely incredulous disbelief all over his
face when I said I didn't mind a bit, I was very glad to be
pregnant, and thank you very much but I'd no intention of
getting married to him or anybody.

There's no getting away from it, it was a very cruel thing to
do. If he'd been an older person, I think I'd have told him all
along I didn't mind how often we went to bed and I wasn't
taking any precautions because I wanted to become pregnant.
But I think if I'd told Malcolm that it would have scared him,
he probably wouldn't have been able to go on doing it. Though

that doesn't entirely salve my conscience; fundamentally I know it's true, I did trick him into it.

For a week or so in the early stages of my pregnancy he came and lived here with me, and that was quite long enough for me to realise clearly that I can't ever live with someone else. I gave most of my time to Peter, and in the evenings I didn't really want to be sociable, I preferred reading. I suppose this is going to sound rather unkind too, but I do feel mentally so much older than Malcolm, which isn't a good thing. Or at least as far as I'm concerned it's not good for a relationship between people because one can't help getting dominant over the other.

I don't see the situation between us changing for the better, either. The simple fact is that Malcolm wants me, me as a person, first and foremost. To get me he's prepared to accept the children, both of them, including Peter who isn't his. But I don't want to be possessed in that way as a person: I want to stay as I am, an individual in my own right and who has two children. He's in love with me very much, and if he had his way I'd be the first person in his life. But he'd never be the first person in mine, I'd put Peter and Jemma and myself before him. So in the long run it couldn't possibly work. I shall stay like I am, and be quite content to.

When I was younger and unhappy, living in one place after another in London with my mother, life always seemed absolutely empty and meaningless then. I never imagined in less than ten years everything would be so totally different. But it is, and in a way which I find very hard indeed to try and describe. . . .

She said, and sat silently for a long time looking out of the window at the bright afternoon of the summer sky, and hearing the sound of the baby on the blanket on the floor by the side of her chair, and lowering her hand towards it.

*

Like the rest of me, everything in this notebook is rambling and untidy and unorganised. I doubt if it's going to be of assistance to you at all. I feel there's so much I've missed out that I ought to have put in; yet if I sit down and try and think what there is that I want to say but haven't, there's nothing at all that comes to mind. I suppose all I can do is give it you as it is and leave it at that, and let you decide whether any of it's any use.

I don't feel I can have been of much help, as I'm not a very definite sort of personality. I wish I was, because I like to think everyone is different in their own way, and not just nothing more than an example of a typical group, and simply a statistic in a vaguely-labelled kind of social group. I wonder if there are any links between unmarried mothers besides the obvious ones? I do hope not.

*

CHAPTER SIX

KATE BYRNE

A man now well sure enough one of those you can forget; but a child is forever.

Kate Byrne had been a nurse for two years at one of the big teaching hospitals in London. At first she was living in the nurses' home, an undistinguished building on the opposite side of the street from it, where she and forty others had identical impersonal rooms into which men were not allowed.

—You see now we couldn't ever be talking freely together could we, with every one else of them there in the communal sitting-room? So it'll have to be like this always, sitting out in the park when I've time off during the day and the weather's nice, or in cafés if it's not; or sometimes if you didn't mind doing it that way we could be sitting somewhere quiet in your car. I'm sorry it's got to be so, but there and that's the regulations they make without exception for us, every one. Sure and you'd think I was a schoolgirl of twelve still wouldn't you, and not a young woman of twenty-four at all.

I wished sometimes that I was the sort to make friends more easily than I do. Then I might be finding another nurse and join up with her, see if we might find a bit of a flat together somewhere. But there's no one here yet so far that I've got to know half well enough at all for anything like that. To be sure and it's no one else's fault but my own, I don't talk to anyone much, in the evenings I mostly stay in the lounge and watch the television, or go up and sit in my room by myself and read and knit.

To be working is the main thing, to make certain that I'm busy all day and got myself as tired as tired can be by the end of it. And not going out either means I'm not for ever spending money on clothes and things so all this time my savings is growing up nicely for me in the bank.

Will we be doing it like that then, are you sure this'll be satisfactory to you? Oh surely and I'll be glad to talk, yes; though I can't help be thinking from what you've told me about it up to now that I'm hardly one who'll fit in with the others somehow anywhere at all. So and if you find at the end that I don't, promise me you'll not worry about it, for sure I shall be understanding it very well indeed if you feel you've no option but to leave me out.

I mean after all I'm different from the other ones, I know that all right. I haven't got any such thing as a baby at all, I haven't, not like them.

*

A white angular face she had, fine boned and with a wide forehead. Her thick Titian-red hair was scraped back over her ears and held tightly at the back of her head with a tiny clasp studded with dully glittering emeralds that matched the greenness of her eyes. Sometimes while she talked she clenched her fists, raising them from time to time and pressing them together tightly between her breasts; at other times almost unthinkingly her abstracted wandering hands slowly unfastened her hair and let it fall free, and she twined the ends of it round between her long white fingers or drew it in thick wine-dark strands across her mouth as though it would muffle the searing anger of the words that spilled endlessly in the softly Irish-accented torrent from the bitter well-spring of her long full lips.

—I was born in the northern part of County Clare, my father had a big farmhouse there, up in the hills where you could see right across to the other side of Galway Bay. A huge great barn of a house with nine or ten bedrooms, far and away the biggest for miles around as befits him as the richest man in the district; and him and my mother and all the rest of the family, every one else of them is still living there to this day. Eight children they have, and all of them alive; I'm the eldest and so far the only one to have left home and moved away.

A very well-off man indeed, my father: he inherited money and married into it too, and he's been a most successful business man on top of it all into the bargain as well. Farming, property, land development, housing, engineering factories, investments abroad; he's always had a real kind of a nose for business, unlike most Irishmen; without a doubt he must have more money than everyone else for fifty miles in any direction all put together, and probably further still than that. None of his children have gone without a thing that they've wanted, that's something he's always boasted could ever be said, if it came to talk of purely material things, that is.

When I was five I had a beautiful Connemara pony for instance, he gave it me for my birthday. A fine long-legged animal, all shiny and wild; and I'd never use a saddle on him to ride him with, he was too splendid and free for that, I'd jump on his back and cling on to his mane like a limpet and the two of us'd go on for ever over the bogs and the fields and the hills like hell. He was black as coal and his name was 'Satan', and a fine pair of devils the two of us made. He had a wicked glint in his eye, and no one ever understood how he felt about the world except me.

Sure and I could be a terrible terror myself all right, and I certainly was, and often too. Tall and skinny and wild and big for my age, and the devil had his home in me all the time. My next youngest sister, Fiona, I remember she annoyed me once, and I picked her up and dumped her in the tub of holy water in the church, and then stood and waited while everybody came running to see what she was screaming and roaring about. I stayed by the door to watch as they lifted her out, so she could see me standing there looking at her all the time and she dursn't say a word about who it was who had put her in. There was another other time too, I remember, when I made up my mind I was going to ride bareback on the big brown bull with a ring through its nose in the top field, and three of my father's men were sent out to come and get me off from it and away. I'd got up on it myself, and I would've got off the same way too, and I cursed them to hell: there was no need for them to come interfering, they could have left me for I'd have ridden it as long as I'd had a mind to and come to no harm.

That was the most important thing of all to me through childhood, I had an absolute mind of my own and a determination to do things, and I hated it whenever other people started telling me what to do instead of leaving me entirely alone. My parents didn't interfere too much, I never had

nothing much to do with either of them at that age; my
mother was preoccupied with the other children and my father
more concerned with business and making money and a position of power for himself, rather than in the endless succession
of children my mother as a good Irish woman bore him with
such unfailing regularity once a year every year for eight
years.

No, my parents weren't my main enemies then: the two
who were in that position to me were the schoolteacher in the
village, and the priest. The schoolteacher was a terrible stupid
woman who ran the little local school, and never taught anyone a word of knowledge of any kind in all her life. All she
knew was to roar at you and shake you if you couldn't recite
your lessons for her like a brainless parrot, and the very first
day I went there she slapped my legs because I wouldn't recite
the prayers with the rest. She was the only teacher there was;
she was supposed to run the school under the supervision of
her husband who was its headmaster, but he was always too far
gone in the drink even to put in an appearance. You could
describe that as the typically Irish educational institution outside of any of the big towns.

The other great idiot one was the priest, an overfed ignora-
mus of a man you had to go to and make your confession on a
Sunday as a child, about stealing sweets and telling lies and all
kinds of ridiculous nonsense of that sort. You were scared of
hell for a day, and then forgot it the rest of the week. My
usual confession was that I'd stole some peppermints from one
of my sisters, though actually I never did in my life because I
couldn't abide the taste of them. But it seemed to satisfy him
all right and he'd pompously give me absolution for it and so
long as it did I couldn't see why I should be bothered to think
up anything else more dreadful for him.

Happy, oh yes I think I was very happy as a child, so long as
I was left alone to enjoy myself. Life was a sort of enjoyably
mischievous song, I remember it mostly as about sunny lakes
and mountain scenery, and roaming around on my own in the
woods and the fields looking for leprechauns, or riding my
pony whenever I got the chance for miles. I was free—no one
impressed themselves on me at all—I think that's a sort of
summary of what I'm trying to say.

Though sure now I see it had its drawbacks, there's no attention or affection I remember ever, from my mother or my father, or from anyone else in the world. And what had been arranged when I was eleven, though it was intended to have exactly the opposite effect on me probably I'm sure, made it all even worse again, all much worse still. I never knew what had hit me until it was too late to alter it or even to try to.

*

—I was sent then to an exclusive and highly fashionable boarding school for girls over the other side of Ireland. It was attached to a convent, and considered to be one of the best that there is, and certainly it's one of the most snobbish and expensive schools for girls in the whole of the country. The fees were nearer two hundred than one hundred pounds a term, which was a very great sum of money to most ordinary people in those days. It was absolutely typical of my father that he should send me there, it shows him exactly for the kind of man he is. It wasn't for my own benefit at all, oh no, I wasn't consulted about it; it was entirely so he could boast among his friends and business connections that unlike the rest of them he was the one who'd got his daughter into there. As I was the eldest child naturally that meant I was the first who became eligible, and therefore I was the first on whom the great privilege was bestowed.

A vast lovely old school it was, a mansion in big grounds of its own in the heart of the country; the best of everything it offered, in education and recreation facilities and food and warmth and clothing. And I hated it all, every single minute of every hour of every day of it, for nearly the whole of the six years that I was there.

I was very backward because of the poor educational grounding I'd had at the village school, and most of all it was the rules and conformity and the whole emphasis of the place that I loathed. For it was all designed to guide you towards discovering you'd got a vocation in life to become a nun. Once a week without fail on a Sunday and every week in the term, we had a long slimy talk from an effeminate priest about the delights of sexual purity and the celibate life, how the greatest achievement a female could aspire to was to become a bride of Jesus Christ. If you couldn't quite reach that standard of self-denial, then the only other alternative was to become the usual complaisant uncomplaining child-bearing cow. According to Irish conventional attitudes, and there aren't any others, those are the only two ways of life open to a woman. So that was what was drilled into you there year after year, the best educational establishment for girls in the land.

I hated it, I detested it, I thought it the most dreadful place in the world with its snobbery and all its nonsense and pretentiousness. The teachers were unintelligent and incapable, and all they did was put on superior airs about what they thought was their own cleverness, and give me the impression they thought I was hopelessly dim. But at that age I wasn't old enough to argue against what my parents had told me, which was that the time had come for me to be properly educated. I didn't know what I wanted to do in life or where I wanted to go, I'd no idea at all what I even wanted to be. Except there was beginning to form inside me, in some vague way I was barely conscious of at all at the time, an incomprehensible and undefined feeling I was determined to be a person. I knew no more than that: somehow I wanted to be somebody definite, with individuality and character and purpose of my own, and have some thing that was mine and no one else's at all.

I must have been fourteen or fifteen I suppose, before the thing happened which seemed from then on to make everything so much clearer to me. On Saturday afternoons we were always allowed to go out from school on the 'bus down to the town, so long as we wore uniform and weren't walking about singly on our own. I was wandering round the market square that particular afternoon with one of the other girls, when all of a sudden out of the corner of my eye I caught sight of a battered old pram standing on its own over near a wall, and apparently no one responsible for it anywhere in sight, or looking after it at all.

I'll not know to this day ever what drew me to it. Even though it was way over the other side of the square I could feel it pulling like a magnet at me, I couldn't resist it, I had to go over to it and see what there was inside. The other girl who was with me, she just followed along, and I don't think she was even conscious of the direction I was taking, that I was making for anywhere or anything special at all. When we got to the pram and I stopped and pulled back the hood so I could look inside of it, she squawked like a frightened hen and turned round and ran away.

But not me, I didn't at all: I just stood there and looked at it, and I thought it was one of the most beautiful sights in all my life I'd ever seen. A hydrocephalic child, monstrous and with a head as big and round and bald as a melon, and filthy with dirt. And I can feel it still now: how all I was conscious of then was a great feeling of yearning for it. I just wanted to pick it up in my arms, and take it away and keep it somewhere hidden and look after it for ever. It seemed as though it had been put there ready for me, waiting for me to come along and take it for my own.

I stood looking at it for how long I don't know at all; and what might have happened or what I might have done if time had gone on and no one had come for it, I've never been able to imagine. I know it seemed like one endless minute after another that I stood there just staring, but of course it was probably nothing whatsoever of the kind. But shortly the child's mother came along, and I'd not think she gave it any thought at all, seeing this schoolgirl standing there by the pram. For all she did was give me a little nod and a smile, and then she wheeled it away and I never saw it again. She can't ever have known the faintest idea how sick I was feeling with disappointment at that moment then, and how envious I was of her for that child.

But from that time onwards I knew without doubt then what it was I wanted; and that it was really something very simple too. It was not some thing, but some body, that would be mine; peculiarly and particularly mine, and not in any way anyone else's at all. Up till then I'd always thought vaguely of it in terms of some kind of skill or training, achieving something nobody else had been able to do. But when I saw that child that afternoon, hideous though it might have been by the world's conventional standards, it came to me as a simple and absolute premonition: what it was to be was a baby of some kind, and whether physically deformed or not was irrelevant. That was what I myself was going to have one day for my own.

After that all the rest of time at school seemed to pass by me in a dream; somehow it never worried or oppressed me at all any more. I even began to take a bit of interest in lessons and to quite enjoy some of them like biology, as though now some

kind of door had been unlocked for me to look through into
the future, and when I'd learned what was waiting for me I
was much more content. I was willing then to let them improve my education as much as they could. I found I enjoyed
reading poetry and listening to music, two things that had
always been without any significance or meaning to me at all
ever before. I can't express it to you any other way: I seemed
at last to have learned the meaning to life, the purpose in it, to
have understood exactly how and where I was going to take
part in it myself and fit in. I wasn't a lost and lonely little
stranger wandering aimlessly through a meaningless maze any
longer; though I'd no idea at all still when it was going to be
that it eventually happened. All I knew was that inevitably it
would. And I was happy to wait however long was necessary
before it did.

I think it was another two years nearly after that before I
realised with the same exact kind of certainty how it was going
to take place. I'd gone home in the summer for the holidays
when I was sixteen and a half. I was still an awkward gangling
adolescent schoolgirl, I blushed furiously every time I was
spoken to by strangers, and didn't know what to say at all in
any kind of conversation with adults.

One Sunday evening a business associate of my father's had
come round to see him, a director of an exporting and ship-
ping company or something like that. I forget where I'd been
out to now, with my mother to see relatives perhaps; and when
we got back to the house she told me to go along to my
father's study to see if he'd be in for the evening meal. When I
knocked on the door and went in the room, this man was
there.

I'd never seen him before, we were briefly introduced and
exchanged a few ordinary formal words of conversation, and I
came away from my father's study again to go back to my
mother in the kitchen. He was over forty, married, not tall or
striking or good looking, or impressive or out of the ordinary
in any way: not in any way unusual or different from dozens
of other men at all. But it was as I was walking along the
passage and crossing the hall that it struck me, again with
absolute certainty, and without the remotest idea of how it
ever possibly could or would happen, that it was by that man

I'd just been introduced to that one day eventually I was going to have my child.

*

—After that I never saw him again nor heard of him, not once for another whole year. I went back to school to get on with my lessons, and soon I'd become a prefect and had a lot more freedom given me then because I was one of the senior girls. I had a nice little room of my own with a dressing-table and wardrobe and wash-basin in it, and was let go down to the town two or three times a week; and so long as you'd got approval for it first from one of the senior mistresses, you were even allowed to go to the dance at the local Catholic church hall where there were boys.

It'd be round about this time that we had the private lessons, individual tuition from the Headmistress herself, that was supposed to tell us the facts of life. It was all mixed together with information about menstruation and periods and how they came about, and the physiological changes in the body that caused them. But it was very late indeed to be giving it us, since all the seniors by then had anyway already been having periods for years. There was no proper teaching about sex or relationships between men and women anywhere in it at all, and certainly no mention ever that there was any such subject as birth control. To be a woman in Ireland meant only one thing then, exactly as it still does now: if you weren't holy enough to be a nun, then God had ordained you a perpetual future as nothing more than a child-bearing machine.

I left school the next year, when I was seventeen and a half. When I went back home it was decided that in the autumn I was to go to Dublin for training as a nurse. That was not my parents' idea, it was something I very much wanted to do myself, become trained or skilled in some way so I'd be able to earn my own living. I wasn't one who was going to stop at home and be nothing but an indolent lady and live on my father all the rest of my life. Though I think he would have preferred me to be that himself, perhaps, which is one of the things made me so determined I wasn't going to do it.

The man I was telling you of, his name was Jack, he was very well in with my father, and often enough at the week-

ends during that summer he was round at our home; he was
always looked upon by my father and mother and everyone
else as an old friend of the family. As I said he was married,
though he had no children of his own. I had little enough
hardly to do with him ever; sometimes I wouldn't catch sight
of him at the house for weeks on end. But always when I did,
if he came for a meal in the evenings with us or something of
that sort, I soon became more and more conscious as time
went on of how often his eyes seemed to be on me. I didn't
know it then, but I've learned it since, it's a well-known fact he
had something almost like a sexual mania as far as young
undeveloped girls were concerned; he was notorious for it in the
district, though of course neither I nor my parents was aware
of the reputation he had for it at the time.

I could tell he was always for ever watching me, when he
was sure no one else was noticing; sometimes I'd look up suddenly when he was in the room and catch the look in his eyes.
I was like a rabbit with a snake, I was; I could feel myself
going hot and cold and quivering all over when I saw what he
was thinking: young and innocent though I was, I knew he
was literally undressing me quite shamelessly and relentlessly
all the time in his mind. And I knew if I was a decent young
lady I should have been affronted and outraged, but I wasn't at
all; I enjoyed it, and I hoped and hoped for the time to come
when he'd actually do it with me in reality.

The first time he ever touched me, the first moment of
physical contact between us, was a Saturday afternoon after
he'd taken me and my mother and two of my sisters out for a
drive in the country with him in his car. We were walking
across the drive at the front of the house, the others had gone
a few steps ahead, and very casually and naturally in what
seemed like an ordinary gesture of friendship just for a moment he held my hand. He must have known immediately
then, from the tremble that shook through the whole of my
body when he did it, that I was going to be one of the easiest
and least resistant conquests he'd ever have made in all his
life.

He went no further that day, and for the rest of the summer
as well he seemed to be in no hurry at all; he knew he didn't
need to be, he enjoyed the certain progress, the leisurely
advancing towards the consummation of it all. A few times he

came round and took me out in his car, sometimes with the
family and once or twice it was on my own; but even on those
occasions he did no more than kiss me tenderly good-bye, and
perhaps allow his hand to lie for a moment or two against my
body and feel the way it signalled its surrender wherever he
chose to touch. He took us all out one time to a dinner and
dance, and I wore an evening dress with a low-cut back; that
was the first time ever he'd held me so he could feel my bare
skin, and I could hardly endure it.

Such a clever man he was, and so experienced; I'll say this
for him to be honest, he was always gentle and considerate in
the way he treated me, the way he slowly taught me with his
caresses there was nothing to be afraid of in sex at all. I'd
never even so much as been kissed by a boy before; he was
most skilled and patient how he initiated me gradually from an
inexperienced virgin schoolgirl into a thoroughly sensual and
fully sexually-experienced female.

It took him all of two years. I suppose it tells a lot for the
patience of his technique that at no time ever did he even so
much as suggest to me he was impatient with my shyness, or
becoming frustrated at my lengthy defence and hesitancies. Of
course it's obvious now, the man was having other women too
at the same time; I can see that now, though no such idea
would ever have crossed my mind then. So he wasn't denying
himself anything at all in the way of sexual satisfaction. In
fact what he must have been enjoying more than anything was
that weird sort of manoeuvring duet that went on between us
for such a long time.

At eighteen or just over, at the beginning of the autumn
anyway, I was accepted by a hospital in Dublin for a two years'
training as a nurse. It meant living-in of course in the hostel
they had for the girls, and my parents were perfectly satisfied I
couldn't come to any kind of harm. There was no arrangement
at all with Jack that he'd come there and see me: but I knew
that he would. And sure enough he did, I'd not been in the
place hardly a week even when a 'phone call came. He told me
with a laugh he had to be in Dublin for a few days to do with
his business, and it had all happened entirely by accident, of
course.

For the whole time of my training we met once every week
at least, and sometimes whenever he could manage it twice or

perhaps even three times. As a student nurse I had to be back
in the hostel always by nine o'clock, so many an evening he'd
call for me in his car as soon as my duty shift was over, and
I'd run straight and change my clothes. Then we'd be off and
away down to the coast, or out into the country to find some
quiet little spot where for an hour or two we could be undis-
turbed in our love-making in the back of his car. But you know
never in all that two years did he go as far as to take my
virginity from me. Everything else though; he'd have the pants
off me, every stitch of clothes from my body, and the both of
us enjoying every erotic game we could put our hands or
minds to. By the time I was nearly twenty-one he'd so
thoroughly aroused me it was me who was for ever begging
him to take me properly, it was me that was pleading for him.
That was how it was, such were the torments of the unsatisfied
physical turmoil he'd so completely and expertly aroused. It
was up to him entirely, to choose his own moment for the
taking of me; he knew he could do it whenever and wherever
he wanted to, without so much as having to say to me even
one more single word.

Still and right up to the time I qualified at the hospital, we
never actually had full sexual intercourse. As soon as I'd passed
my examination I went home for a short holiday to celebrate it
with my parents. While I was there, Jack came, playing his
part of the old friend of the family, he used that as the excuse
one day to drop in and see me. I couldn't help myself; as soon
as we were alone together in the room I was in his arms, we
were kissing each other totally oblivious of everything else
when my father unexpectedly came back in.

Then, oh there was the most terrible riot this side of hell. My
father was roaring and shouting like a madman and ordered
Jack out of the house; me, I was screaming and swearing and
saying I didn't care at all for convention, I was going away
with him, we were going to live together for ever for the rest of
our lives as man and wife. So Jack went off, and my father still
cursed me for a whore and a strumpet, he said he'd give me a
home no longer; I was to pack my cases at once, and when I
had he drove me straight away to the station for to get the
next train back to Dublin.

Of course Jack hadn't gone to his home, he knew exactly
what would happen; and when I came out of the railway

station in Dublin, there he was, already and waiting for me in the forecourt with his car. The hospital were not expecting me to come back from my holiday for another couple of weeks, so I couldn't turn up at the hostel there. But Jack said a friend of his had lent him the key of a flat over the other side of the city near Phœnix Park; the friend was not using it himself because he was off on business for several months ahead. So we could go there together if we liked and stay.

So that was where I found out what physical love between a man and a woman really was then; it seemed no more than the natural completion of something we'd allowed interruption to take place in always before. Love, love; I loved him, I wanted him so desperately, so violently it became like a drug I couldn't live without. For days and nights without end almost we stayed in bed and made love together a dozen, two dozen, fifty, oh I've no idea at all how many times. I only knew I wanted him to go on and on.

'*Naked I wait thy love's uplifted stroke . . .*' Do you know *The Hound of Heaven*? They say it's supposed to be about God, but it's never seemed so to me, it hasn't; it's just exactly as I was then, the state I was in at that time:

> '*Naked I wait Thy love's uplifted stroke,*
> *My harness piece by piece Thou hast hewn from me,*
> *And smitten me to my knee;*
> *I am defenceless utterly.*'

Sure and he was the first man ever to me, I'd known nothing and no one at all before: and he knew so well how to give me pleasure. It takes a long time to arouse an innocent girl and teach her the arts of making love and to be unembarrassed about it, but he did it yet he treated me all the time without fail like I was a china doll.

When he had to go out to get food, or make 'phone calls to do with his business, I'd lie in bed helpless and wait for him to come back; my whole body seemed on fire for him, scarcely able to keep still until he'd returned. I'd no idea what it was he'd done to me; only that he'd changed me from whatever it was I'd been into a woman to whom sex and the enjoyment of it were everything, simply everything that there was in the world.

I knew I couldn't give it up, I could think of nothing else at all; while I was there at the flat I rang up the hospital and told them I'd have to stop off another fortnight because I was ill. For a few days soon after, Jack had to go away back to his home to attend to some business matters; and I spent a terrible miserable time on my own in the flat, not daring to go out in case he should come back and not find me there, and all the time just sitting yearning and crying for him, not able to sleep or eat or do anything at all. When he did come back, by then I'd got the most terrible menstrual period on, so then I still couldn't have him until it was done. And I didn't know it at that time either, but it was the last one I'd have till a long time afterwards again.

He was very very restless when he came back; I thought at first it was because we couldn't make love due to my period, but when it was over he was still the same. I'd no idea at all what it was could be on his mind. He said he had a lot of work to do, he was getting behind with things in his business, and he took to spending more and more time away during the day and staying out of the flat. Whatever it was, I didn't know or want to: all I wanted was him.

But it couldn't go on as it had been doing: even I, besotted as I was, wanting nothing else than to be made love to all day by him, could understand it couldn't continue like that. At last I asked him one afternoon if he'd drive me up to the hospital, so I could see Matron and arrange with her about when I should begin working again. Just as he was turning the car in at the main gates he said to me, casually as you please, that if she wanted me to start back right away, I should tell her I could begin any time, the following day even, if that was what she wanted me to do.

I knew, and so did he, that if she did it could mean only one thing: me moving out of the flat at once the very next day and back into the nurses' hostel. So it was all done then, and just like that: our living and loving all day was ended, and the flame blown out with a few words as meaninglessly as though it was just a used-up match.

By the following night I was in residence again in the hospital as a junior staff nurse, and I was given my own cold and gloomy little room. Jack said he'd go back home for a few days; then he'd come over to Dublin again for a week and we would get together for a good long talk, to see if there wasn't some kind of permanent arrangement for being together we could make.

A week went by, a fortnight, three weeks; I never heard a word from him. In the fourth week I suddenly realised something else too that had happened: I'd missed my period, a thing which had never occurred in all my life before. Birth control I knew nothing of at all; my ideas of it were vague, and the practice had been totally non-existent as far as I was concerned. To me it was sufficient to rely on it that Jack was a much older and more experienced man; I'd never even discussed it with him, I trusted him completely. I'd not thought about it scarcely at all, I'd always put the whole subject out of my mind as something that would only spoil the beauty of what was between us.

For a day or two I tried to persuade myself it was probably only because I'd been indulging in intercourse with such regularity and violent exertion that I'd upset the normal physiological processes of my body. If I didn't worry about it, eventually it was bound to come on, then everything would be all right again. But as time went by and it didn't, the terrible truth of the matter began to dawn on me with all the horror of a nightmare, that I was pregnant.

I sent a telegram to Jack at his place of business, very short and uninformative, asking him please to come and see me as soon as he could. No reply. I waited a few more days, then I sent another one, rather more urgently phrased. Still no answer. I tried to ring him at his business number, at home and at one of his other factories. One place they said he was in Limerick, somebody else said he was in Sligo, somebody else that he'd had to go over to London for a few days.

I was desperate and so terrified and lonely. But most of all I was in the horror that all Irish girls face. Because of my upbringing and conditioning, all my education and background, all the priest-ridden hypocritical ignorant society that I'd lived in all through my life, I was filled to the depths of my soul with a terrible feeling of complete and utter degradation and shame.

*

Time went by, and in that time she moved from the nurses' home into a small bed-sitting room, expensive because it had its own dining-alcove and kitchenette; it was one she could only just afford.

—Eight guineas is a lot of money to be paying for a tiny bit of a place like this to be sure, but at least I've got my own key. I thought I would because it's self-contained and I can come and go as I please. The bit of money I saved by putting in the Post Office while I was living in at the hospital, I'll slowly buy a few nice pieces of furniture of my own for it to try and make it look more like a proper home, and maybe a few new clothes for myself too while I'm about it.

My cases I've brought over from the nurses' home, I haven't properly unpacked them yet, you must excuse me how I look in this old darned jumper and skirt, it's the first thing I pulled out to wear when I moved in. The rest of my clothes can wait, I don't suppose there'll be much of an occasion for them.

I don't go out at all anywhere, I've no extravagances, nothing of any kind except a bit of food and a tiny drop to drink now and again. Now that's put me in mind of something, it has: look here what I bought from my pay-packet I got on Thursday, down at the off-licence place at the corner. Will I be making you some coffee then, real Irish coffee I mean, with plenty of this whiskey to it and the cream? I was going to do it for myself, but go on and let me do it for you as well, you can join me in the little sort of a celebration that I've got this place for myself to live. Here's two nice glasses for us, see.

What you'd have in a restaurant you know, would only be an apology for it, this that I'll make for us you won't forget it I promise, it'll be the real true thing. We can go on with the talking though through most of the time I'd doing it, until we get to the little bit difficult part.

Just be reminding me now how far it was last time that we'd got. Oh yes Jack and his disappearing and that; well I never did find out the truth behind all that business ever really at all. He turned up again eventually in Dublin a few weeks later, with some lame sort of a tale about having been so busy catching up with his work that he'd had to neglect everything else till it was done. I don't believe a word of it; if you ask me what

I truly think, I think he'd got himself another young girl already by then tucked away somewhere, and he'd been spending most of his time with her.

When I told him how it was with me, that I was pregnant I mean, he took it as cool as you please. Not to worry my head about it he said, he could get me just the very tablets for it that'd take it away. He didn't grasp I was already near three months gone by them; and of course the tablets when he brought them made not an atom of difference at all.

Abortions are out of the question altogether in Ireland. Jack said the only thing I could do then was stay on at work in the hospital as long as I could, and he'd give me the money to come over here to England with, where I could have the baby and then put it for adoption. It was as clear as anything could be he wasn't in the least interested at the idea of a baby, in fact he thought it a downright nuisance, that was all. It'd not come into his mind even, that I might have feelings about it myself and would want to keep it. How could he know it was all part of something that started inside me six years or more before, when I was at school and I'd seen the baby that day I told you of in the market square in its pram?

Well it's ready and this is the most important moment now, watch very carefully and look what I do. The plenty of sugar in the bottom of the glass, and the strong black coffee poured onto it very hot, with the spoon in it like that to stop the glass breaking. Then we put in a really good big pour of whiskey like this, sure it's not worth drinking at all unless the whiskey's as much as the coffee nearly. Stir it up well and then there we are; and this next is the bit now where you need to have a steady hand. I put the dessert-spoon, bowl upwards on top of it, like that; and then pour the cream slowly as this, ever so slowly and gently now over it so that it slides down softly like that and floats on the coffee and covers it all over. There now, that's it. Have a taste of it, go on then, tell me did you ever before experience anything in your life quite like that? Sure and if I had the money to spend on such things I'd be drinking it always every day myself, I'd ask for nothing else out of life I wouldn't. Well I'm glad you like it, when you've finished it I'll be happy to make another one for you as many times as you wish. Now I'll make one for me too.

I was telling you, wasn't I, how I hadn't the intention of

going to London at all? Instead I went to a private doctor in Dublin, and that was the most terrible mistake I made ever in the whole of my life. I'd gone to him thinking he was going to help find a place for me to have my baby in a private nursing home; but instead of that he straightaway passed my name to a big Catholic organisation for fallen women and before I could even turn round a priest from them was up at the hospital. No discretion or secrecy, asking for me by name and telling the Matron where he belonged to, so there was no need at all for her even to wonder why a priest should suddenly arrive out of the blue like that and be wanting to see me.

And a long long talk I had from him, the smarmy devil; all about what a wonderful place they had down near the west coast, where I could go to have my baby and the both of us would be well looked after. I told him flat there and then that I wanted to keep it, and of course I could, of course he said; but it was too early yet to come to any definite decision at all of that kind. Naturally I wouldn't want my parents to know about it, he said, so if I'd just leave it all to them everything would be taken care of in the nicest and quietest and best possible way.

You have to remember at the time I'm telling you of, although I'd lived like a kept woman those few weeks in the flat with Jack, apart from that I was really the most innocent creature there ever could be. I'd had the best education possible for a girl in Ireland at an expensive boarding school, which meant I'd learnt absolutely nothing whatsoever of the realities of the world, and had no training at all in how to even begin to think for myself. The opposite, in fact; for it had all prepared me for being a true Irish woman, subservient and biddable, believing men were superior creatures and among them priests were the finest and holiest and most noble of them all.

This was the sort of thing that priest did; he said he'd have a quiet word with the Matron of the hospital, he thought he could talk her into letting me stay on until I could work no longer, and then I could go straight down and stay in the organisation's home until after my baby was born. Since it was him coming there had made it plain to everyone I must be pregnant, a great favour he was doing me I'm sure in making such a generous offer of that kind.

Jack came by to see me from time to time, and still sometimes even he took me out. When he did it was only because he wanted one thing. But I loved him so much even then, and I let him go ahead and do it in the back seat of his car, though I was six months pregnant or more and it hurt like hell. When it came when I was seven months or just over, I couldn't go on: the work at the hospital was tiring me out and though I knew it meant not seeing Jack again for two or three months, I felt I had to get away and go down to the mother and baby home where I could rest.

I was soon disillusioned about that little dream too when I got there. A great gloomy place like an old army barracks it was, high walls all around and poky little rooms with filthy small windows high up that you couldn't see out of, and had never been opened for a hundred years if you were to judge by the smell. An army place, a convent, a prison, whatever it had been it would have been ideal for any of those; but it certainly wasn't a suitable place for unmarried girls to go to for having their babies. It was run by the fiercest and most sour-faced nuts of nuns you could ever imagine. They had us down on our knees all day, washing and polishing the floors, and scrubbing: then we had a short break now and again, so we could all get up from our work in time to kneel down again and say a prayer of thanks together to God for all the kindnesses that were being showered on us there.

And it was ten pounds a week that they charged us for the privilege of stopping in the place, and about twenty pounds' worth of work they had from you in exchange. There were a hundred girls there altogether, and one midwife for the lot of them, and not a single doctor of any kind ever came into the place. We slept in long cold dormitories, the beds in rows and the nuns patrolling all night up and down between to do their nursing, which consisted of hissing at everyone who dared make a sound, and telling her to keep quiet else she'd wake up everyone else.

The babies were taken away every night and put in a nursery over the far side of the building so no one could see them or hear them. What sort of conditions they were kept in I don't know, but I remember one girl got in because she wanted to see her own child and came back in a desperate state, crying because she'd seen all the babies lying two and three huddled together in each cot.

What small savings I had were going down rapidly, and I wanted to get the birth of my own child over, and to be out and away from that place as soon as I could. When I had the chance I laid my hands on some salts kept in one of the store-rooms in the corridor at the end of the dormitory, and took a bloody great dose of them that nearly blew my guts out. But it did the trick; I went into labour three weeks earlier than I should have, and gave birth to my boy prematurely. His weight was just five and a half pounds, and I called him John.

I wasn't allowed to see much of him hardly at all; we could only have our babies with us an hour in the morning and an hour in the afternoon. The whole idea of that place was aimed towards one thing only, though I'd no idea what it was at the time. It was nothing else but adoption; and from what I've heard since the majority of babies adopted through the Church in Ireland come all from that home, nearly every single one.

Hardly had I had John then the pressure began; sometimes I used to think they must have got it all worked out on a sort of rota system. No matter what time of day it was or where you were, never an hour went by without you hearing from some-one, either a nurse or a priest or a nun, to the effect that you'd been a disgrace to your family: but they themselves would stand by you. You need have no fear: as soon as the adoption formalities were settled there'd be no more trouble, your family would be persuaded to relent and take you back.

It was wicked, wicked it was; and on and on it went, day after day. You're in no state at all to go on putting up a fight, it eats at your will, nibbles it away bit by bit until you feel you've hardly got a thought left to call your own in your head. Somehow temporarily at least I managed to hang on; I kept telling myself I was damned if I was going to let them do to me what I'd seen them do to the others, I'd do anything I could think of to see them all in hell first.

But the longer I hung on the less my money was getting, since I was paying for my baby's keep there as well as my own. I remembered what Jack had said about giving me money to go over to England to get the baby adopted, so I wrote and asked him if he would keep his promise now, and send me sufficient to go with. I didn't tell him I wouldn't be taking the baby with me when I went, because I thought he might guess I'd no intention then of trying to place it in London for adoption at all, which of course I hadn't.

He sent me the money, and with it a letter to say if he ever came over to London I could rely on it he'd get in touch with me. He made it quite clear, not by what he said but by all the things he missed out, that he didn't have a single shred of feeling anywhere in him any more at all for me. It was strange, but somehow I'd been expecting it, and it seemed hardly to touch me or hurt me at all. I didn't care for Jack any longer, and I realised I hadn't done so since before the baby was born. All the love I'd got left in me was utterly and entirely and only for John.

When the money arrived I told them at the home I was away off to England to find myself a job, and as soon as I'd got one I'd be coming back to take my baby. They turned round then and said that wasn't ever allowed; it'd have to go for temporary adoption until I returned because they had no facilities there for keeping babies without their mothers. If I didn't agree to that, then the only alternative would be to have him put in an orphanage.

Since they swore it was only a temporary adoption, and gave me a paper to sign and pointed out very carefully to me where it was printed on it this was only to last for six months, I agreed. I came to England then, to London, thinking I'd been given my freedom and in a few weeks time I'd have found a job and a home to live in for me and my baby.

It's hard for anyone to believe, I suppose, the ignorance that still exists in Irish girls in this day and age. London was like no city I'd ever imagined on earth, huge and teeming with people and very frightening. But what was much more serious and worse was I soon found the nursing training I'd had in Ireland wasn't sufficient to get me a decent job in a hospital here, and be able to afford what it cost to live outside it in a place of my own.

Though by then I'd little enough faith left in me, the only people I could think to turn to were one of the Catholic societies over here to help homeless and friendless girls. I should have known better than to do what I did, which was I went and put my problem to them, laid all my cards on the table and asked if they could assist me in what I was trying to do. Oh to be sure they could, they said; I was not to worry myself one bit, it'd take them no time at all to have everything straightened out. They found nice comfortable digs for me, a room I shared with another girl in a house full of other good Catholic girls, and all of us under the wing of a specially-chosen woman who was there to befriend us and look after us and see we came to no harm.

The devils; for behind my back they straight away wrote to my parents and the first I knew of it was when I had a letter from my father telling me never again to come home. Behind my back they communicated with the home in Ireland too where I'd been to have my baby, and made sure it'd gone away from there for adoption. But to my face they sent a jolly young priest to see me three times a week, who told me he'd been specially assigned to devote himself and the whole of his energies to the helping of me.

He was very clever; oh yes, those Irish Catholic bastards, so were they all. Under the guise of caring for me and acting as my adviser and friend, he persuaded me the best thing to do would be to take a year's further training in hospital here, so that I could build myself up into a really independent financial position and then bring my baby over and afford to have some-one in to look after it for me while I worked.

Depressed and lonely and worried like I was, and missing my baby all the time and wondering where he was and what was happening to him, I got so I could do nothing but sit around all day, I could hardly even drag myself to the hospital where I was supposed to begin work. So the friendly priest came to the rescue again, to take me to see a very good Catholic doctor; a first class psychiatrist he said he was reputed to be, who was very kind and experienced at helping girls through difficult times after they'd had their babies.

The help he gave me was pills, and to this day what they did or were, I'll never know. Anti-depressants and tranquillisers I suppose, but so many and in such heavy doses I was walking round all day like a zombie, going wherever and doing what-ever I was told. They were all of them in it together, every single one: my parents, the mother and baby home, the psychiatrist doctor, the society here and the young priest who was its representative. All combining to bring about that one ultimate end; what chance could a girl on her own have against an array like that?

It was one afternoon that the priest came and told me there were a few simple legal documents needed signing, down in the City at a lawyer's office, they were to do with financial arrangements between myself, my parents and the people who were looking after my baby. When I got there I was given a whole sheaf of papers, they were put before me endlessly one after another on the desk. I tried to read each one at first, but the print was swimming in front of my eyes there was so much of the drugs in me; after I'd struggled through the first three or four I was so tired with the effort I gave up trying, and as they produced them I just signed and signed.

It was weeks later, when I was beginning to feel better and was taking the drugs much less, that I started to enquire from the priest and his organisation exactly how the legal position stood. It was then that I discovered what it was that I'd done; all its implications and results, and the impossibility of un-doing it again in any way. One of the papers I'd signed had been the second and final part of the adoption agreement. John was my baby no longer, I'd given up all my rights and claims. I couldn't ever see him again, or know what had become of him or even where he was; he didn't belong to me any more at all.

Chalk-faced and drawn-featured, she let her arms drop limp by the sides of her chair; she laid her head back and closed her eyes, and sat inanimate and drained. On the table in front of her the Irish coffee in her long stemmed glass stood forgotten; untouched, untasted, cold.

*

As she began to earn more money she bought occasional things like a bedside lamp, a brightly striped seersucker table-cloth, some royal blue cotton curtains. And sometimes she even spent some of her wages on clothes. A tightly fitting white lambswool sweater once, and with it a short white kid leather skirt, which she wore with thick cream tights of ribbed wool woven with silver lurex, and small square-toed black patent leather shoes with large white buckles.

And she sat alone in her room in the evenings and smoked cigarettes and drank whiskey, and read a book or did her

knitting. Whatever she wore, always jangling on her wrist was
a gold chain-bracelet, and dangling from it nine miniature
golden charms.

—Oh this, I always wear it, I always have. It's a kind of
reminder to me, a sort of perpetual warning of my individual
weaknesses. Each one of them has a special significance and
meaning to it; they were all given me to mark different occasions with Jack, and they all except one came from him. You
can follow the steps in our relationship if you take them as
they're arranged round in order, one by one. See now: first a
pair of hands clasped together, then a rose-petal, after that an
apple, a half-opened book, and then a heart. A little pony, it's
obvious what that was for now isn't it, then a turf-cutter's
cottage and lastly the crescent of a moon. Then next to that
the final one that I bought myself: a fortune teller's crystal
ball, in a cradle. The story of four years of my life there; that
all began with a man, but isn't ended yet. A man now well sure
enough one of those you can forget; but a child is forever, so
that's why I keep them all, to show me how it came.

My new outfit tonight, you like it do you, yes I'm glad. I
have the feeling one day there'll be a fine young fellow walks
into my life, you know how I mean? Walk into my parlour
said the spider to the fly; if he's the right sort of boy for me I'll
see to it he hasn't a chance to get away. Shall I tell you what I
really am? I'm a witch with a black, black heart. I'm like a
leech too, if I make up my mind to start something I'll go on
with it right to the very end, even if it's necessary to kill someone on the way. Yes, I have come to a decision. I've decided I
can't sit back here for ever and wait for things to happen any
more. I'm going to make them happen; and so they will sure
enough, if I'm determined to make it that they shall.

Yesterday, do you know what yesterday was? It was the
third birthday of my son John. Three years old he is now: and
I don't know where he is or who's got him or how I could
begin to try to get him back. I know one thing though, and one
thing only: which is by Jesus God that I will.

Listen, you have no idea what I'd do, what lengths I'd go to
to get him. I mean it, I'd do anything, anything of any kind at
all. I'll go to mass, I'll go to confession, I'll find me a good
Catholic boy with money to marry in a Catholic church, then

I'll go back to Ireland with him to show them I'm a properly married woman now, and I'm there for what is mine by right, which is my child. And then when I finally get him they can all go straight out of the window to hell: the Church, the priests, the husband I've got, and every man else in the whole of the world. I'm full up to here where my heart was with hate for them; my father, every man there is anywhere, because they've taken part of my body from me, and nothing will satisfy me ever now until I get it back.

And I don't care how many men I have to fight, and how, and for how long. I'll use every weapon there is, my brain, my sex, my body against them; seduce them, fight them with my bare fists, whatever way I can best hurt them, that's all I have a mind to do to them now until I win in the end. That priest was always telling me to forget; at my age with my looks I was one of the lucky ones, he said. But he didn't know, no one knows, the fire that's burning inside me, cold as ice sometimes and other times like the flames of hell. And while I wait I try to stop myself thinking and try to keep myself busy with something to occupy my hands, like this.

*

She laid down her knitting across her knee, smoothing it softly with her fingers, tracing its outline: a pale lilac-blue matinée coat exactly right in size for a baby six months of age.

72 73 10 9 8 7 6 5 4 3 2 1